Burn for
Christ Just . . .
Don't Burn Out!

CHI ENG YUAN

WESTBOW
PRESS®
A DIVISION OF THOMAS NELSON
& ZONDERVAN

WestBow Press books may be ordered through booksellers or by contacting:

WestBow Press
A Division of Thomas Nelson & Zondervan
1663 Liberty Drive
Bloomington, IN 47403
www.westbowpress.com
1 (866) 928-1240

ISBN: 978-1-9736-5828-3 (sc)
ISBN: 978-1-9736-5827-6 (e)

Library of Congress Control Number: 2019903679

Print information available on the last page.

WestBow Press rev. date: 04/15/2019

Foreword

Dr. Chi-Eng Yuan is the perfect person to write a book about burning for Christ without burning out. He is a first-generation Chinese immigrant to the United States who has spent most of his adult life in ministry in North America, particularly to the Chinese church here. I first met him when I started teaching at Denver Seminary thirty years ago. He was a beginning theological student; I was a rookie professor. He had a wonderful ministry in a Chinese church in Denver for many years, where I was privileged to speak on numerous occasions. But he burned out. Like so many pastors of any ethnicity he was involved in so many good things. How does one say no to ministry when it is personally rewarding and obviously helping others? The challenge is perennial and today it seems we have a record number of casualties.

Dr. Yuan could have quit. Like others, he could have abandoned his calling and found a secular job and made more money than he ever has in ministry. His amazing wife Kar-Shan stuck with him when more fragile marriages would undoubtedly have broken apart. He got help from counselors, denominational leaders, and took time away from ministry for refreshment, rejuvenation and refocus, and not just for a few weeks or months. He enrolled in Denver Seminary again and earned his D.Min. to complement the M.Div. he earned years earlier. Appropriately, he did his research and wrote his thesis on the phenomenon of burnout in ministry, especially among the Chinese evangelical Christian community. There are certain traits in East Asian cultures that perhaps exacerbate the possibility of burnout, though there is also intense cultural pressure not to acknowledge it, to put on a good front, and slog it out indefinitely even when one's heart and spirit have long since gone elsewhere. Dr. Yuan resisted these cultural pressures. Today he and his wife travel North America and China in an itinerant ministry of preaching, teaching, consulting and encouraging pastors, churches and entire denominations. His ministry is more balanced and therefore stronger than it ever was previously. He has more input, guidance, sounding boards and accountability than ever before. Dr. Yuan writes this book from experience and from a position of complete credibility.

The topics of this book are also exactly what are needed in a primer on burnout. Solid biblical exegesis and theological reflection informs everything that appears here. Dr. Yuan does not prooftext, nor does he present a philosophy and then try to baptize it by finding Scriptures that might in part match it. He spent countless hours poring over the Old and New Testaments; I know because I was his second reader for his D.Min. thesis and the person responsible for supervising the biblical and theological side of his research. More than once I sent him back to the Bible to do more work! But neither does Dr. Yuan stop with the biblical worlds and texts. He asks what must be done to bring their principles into the twenty-first century with all its multiculturalism and complexity. Perhaps at least as significant is that unlike so much therapeutic writing, the result is not that the reader senses the need just to cut back and take life easier. We need to be involved in kingdom activity as much as ever, with a burning passion for the things of Christ, as the title to the book indicates. We simply need to work smarter rather than harder, with rhythms of work and rest, devotion and service that fit our unique gifting and circumstances.

Readers will therefore find no program, no formula, no one-size-fits-all model of burning for Christ without burning out, in this gem of a book. They will have to take the texts, principles, illustrations and suggestions and apply them to their own contexts and settings. They will have to depend on God and godly counsel. But they will have no lack of ideas for what they might do in the process. This book deserves a wide audience. Read it with delight and gratitude for God's grace and gifting and in hopes of being able to serve him as best as you possibly can—which almost by definition means qualitatively not quantitatively. Thank you, Chi-Eng, for your labor of love in taking your research and putting it in this most accessible and helpful form. And to God be the glory.

Craig L. Blomberg, Distinguished Professor of New Testament, Denver Seminary, Littleton, COLORADO, USA

This book is about burning and passionate zeal for Christ. It covers all the ingredients for any pastors who want to serve the Lord for a life time without burn out or drop out from the ministry. It is comprehensive and inclusive. It is biblical and practical. It is also essential as the "spiritual vitamins" for sustaining a pastor's ministry that includes spirituality, competence, rest, conflict management, culture adaption and having a confidant.

—-Dr. Chuck Raup

It is well-researched with a good use of Biblical illustrations. It is also well-written and clear with many practical helps. Yuan have analyzed pastoral burnout in a helpful way, and offer good counsel for dealing with burnout.The book deserves to be read not only by pastors, but by lay leaders in the church as well.

—-Ken Swetland, Senior professor of ministry,
Gordon Conwell Theological Seminary

Yuan takes a candid yet caring look at how those in pastoral ministry can guard against the all-too-frequent reality of burn-out. His research is thorough and his help is wise, offering solid biblical guidance in how to feed continually on God's strength while practicing healthy relationships and rhythms of living. This book will light the path to vibrant and joy-filled ministry that endures. Read it, and then read it again.

—Brenda Quinn, Pastor of Spiritual Formation
Living Way Fellowship Church

"Chi-Eng Yuan's book *Burn for Christ, just... **Don't Burn Out!** provides biblical examples of burnout, presents different causes of burnout, and gives preventative actions to avoid burnout— or cure it when it happens. Pastors will see themselves many places in the book. I recommend it for the helpful insights that it provides.*"

—Dr. David Osborn
Senior Professor of Christian Leadership of Denver Seminary, Colorado, USA

To my dearest Heavenly Father,

Thank you for choosing the name "Chi Eng" for me— 奇恩 (in Chinese) which means Amazing Grace.

Thank you for molding my life as a journey of your Amazing Grace.

"I love you, O Lord, my strength." (Psalm 18:1 NIV)

"… Who am I, O Sovereign God, …that you have brought me this far?." (2 Samuel 2:18 NIV)

The only focus of the rest of my life is burn for Christ but just do not burnout.

To my lovely wife: Kar-Shan, whom I am dedicating this book to you. (* The first draft of this book has been a gift from Chi Eng to Kar-Shan for their 30-years wedding anniversary on March 27, 2012.)

Thank you for your being my beloved and my confidant. Your are my treasure of noble character from my Heavenly Father. Your reflection of God's unconditional love towards me since the first day we fell in love. Your path of caring and supporting me day by day and year by year has deepened me to love God and to love you more.

Acknowledgement

Dr. Chuck Raup
Thank you for being the first reader for my thesis. Your questions challenged me to think and write from different perspective. Your insight helped me to refine the content from the first word to the last phrase. I feel more thankful that you become my lifelong mentor in Christ.

Dr. Craig Blomberg
Thank you for encouraging me to do my best to make known precisely and concisely the biblical truth of this book. Thank you for sharpening my theological mind and also expanding my horizon of digging in knowing God's Word. Thank you for your support in different seasons of my life.

Mark Buchanan
Thank you for your willingness to spend hours and hours editing the first draft of this book. Your professional perspective and brotherhood kindness reduced my anxiety and improved my foreseeing the finishing line of this project.

Win Stanford
Thank you for helping me to edit the final draft of this book. You and your husband, John Stanford are wonderful ministry partners for me and my wife, Kar-Shan. I appreciate your effort in getting this book to finish well in the finishing line.

1

Introduction

Welcome to the journey, toward renewed passion for serving the Lord, and away from the exhaustion of repeated burnout. I myself have experienced burnout firsthand, and also rekindled passion to take up my cross and follow Christ wholeheartedly.

Have you experienced burnout? You are not alone. In the last four decades, burnout among pastors has become epidemic. Research reveals a cause-and-effect relationship between burnout and leaving the ministry. Gary McIntosh, in *It Only Hurts on Monday*, cited the results of a survey of pastors who had recently left the ministry and concluded that 40 percent had experienced some form of burnout. Berkeley professor Christina Maslach, in *Maslach Burnout Inventory Manual*, identified three major indicators of burnout: "Emotional exhaustion, experienced as fatigue caused by extensive interaction with others, depersonalization, characterized by development of an uncaring and cynical attitude toward others, and lack of personal accomplishment, indicated by deterioration of self-confidence and decreased personal satisfaction with one's achievement."

Based on Maslach's definition, pastoral burnout is a state or process of fatigue and frustration, brought on by maintaining a distance from God, others and ourselves, which can be measured as increased emotional exhaustion, progressive depersonalization of the congregation, and a decreased sense of personal accomplishment.

Burnout accumulates over time and can be accompanied by a range of adverse physical and psychosomatic symptoms. By way of illustration, few years ago, an internal survey by the Evangelical Lutheran Church in America found that 69 percent of ministers reported being overweight, 64 percent had high blood pressure, and 13 percent were taking antidepressants.

Burnout is a serious problem not only among American pastors but also among pastors in other parts of the world. Rein Brouwer, lecturer in practical theology at Protestant Theological University of Utrecht, Netherlands, comments that, "Burnout is an occupational hazard for Dutch pastors as well. Pastors suffer from an overload of work pressure, organizational conflicts, and lack of support, often culminating in extended periods of stress and burnout."

No pastor, regardless of race or ministry, is immune to burnout. Black pastors in America, for example, suffer from burnout by tending to let their congregation off the hook by doing all of the work, as well as their own public ministry, by themselves. Members of such congregations delight in the involvement of the pastor, but feel no personal obligation themselves to serve in the church. Furthermore, many Korean-American pastors get into difficulty quickly because of unrealistic goals. They strive for highly abstract goals that are almost impossible to reach. These goals are often vague, making it hard to know if the goal *has* been reached. Many pastors work diligently toward this ideal only to feel frustrated and defeated. Even when they see some progress, their ideal is never reached, and perceived failure often leads inevitably to burnout.

Basic Definition of Burnout

In discussing burnout, its causes and consequences, it is important to have a working definition. Wilmar Schaufeli and Dirk Enamann offer a helpful definition of burnout:

> Burnout is a persistent, negative, work-related state of mind in "normal" individuals that is primarily characterized by exhaustion, which is accompanied by distress, a sense of reduced effectiveness, decreased motivation, and the development of dysfunctional attitudes and behaviour at work. This psychological condition develops gradually but may remain unnoticed for a long time by the individual involved.[1]

The Bible uses "heart" to describe the seat of emotions.[2] The Hebrew word for heart is *lēb*,[3] appearing more than eight hundred times in the Old Testament.[4] "Heart" is the term applied to "the totality of man's inner or immaterial nature, in general, to one of the three traditional personality functions of man: emotion, thought, or will. The whole spectrum of emotion is attributed to the heart."[5]

---

[1] Wilmar Schaufeli and Dirk Enzmann, *The Burnout Companion to Study & Practice* (Philadelphia, PA: Taylor & Francis, 1998), 36.

[2] Heinz-Josef Fabry, "lēb," in *Theological Dictionary of the Old Testament*, vol.7, ed. G. J. Botterweck, H. Ringgren, and H.-J. Fabry (Grand Rapids: Eerdmans, 1977), 414.

[3] Ibid., 400.

[4] Marjorie O'Rourke Boyle, "The Law of the Heart: the Death of a Fool (I Samuel 25)," *Journal of Biblical Literature* 120 (2001): 401. See Hans W. Wolff, who counts 858 instances (*The Anthropology of the Old Testament* [trans. Margaret Kohl; London: SCM, 1974], 40).

[5] Andrew Bowling, "Heart, Understanding, Mind," in *Theological Wordbook of the Old Testament*, vol. 2, ed. R Laird Harris, Gleason Archer, and Bruce Waltke (Chicago: Moody, 1980), 466.

Basson agrees that in the OT the heart is considered not just the seat of emotions but also of "personality, rationality and volition."[6] In Greek, the word for heart is kardia, which appears 160 times in the New Testament. It denotes the center of all physical and spiritual life.[7] In other words, the heart is "the person in its totality"[8] and consists of the different intellectual, spiritual and emotional functions of a person. Consequently, when the pastor's heart is exhausted and in danger, the pastor's whole life and entire ministry will also be threatened.

Burnout features "loss of energy, loss of enthusiasm and loss of confidence"[9] in a job or work environment. The Bible begins with Adam's responsibilities in the Garden of Eden "to work it and take care of it." (Gen 2:15 NIV) The OT boasts an extensive vocabulary of *work*. The words express the awareness that work is invariably both a blessing and a curse after the fall, because since then human beings have had to perform a disproportionate amount of work, even to meet their basic needs.

So what is God's original plan for work? Mead explains that:

> The biblical word for labor conveys various types and meanings of work, ranging from physical and mental toil to the products of labor. The Bible affirms the goodness of labor, the hope for reward despite its burdens, and the potential for dishonest gain or cruel enslavement. Theologically, the pattern for all human labor is God's work of creation, taught in

---

[6] Alec Basson, "Metaphorical Explorations of the Heart in the Old Testament," *Scriptura* 96, no. 2 (2007): 310.

[7] Theo Sorg, "Heart," in *The New International Dictionary of New Testament Theology*, ed. Colin Brown, vol. 2 (Grand Rapids: Zondervan, 1979), 180-84.

[8] Ibid., 181.

[9] Michael P. Leiter and Christina Maslach, *Banishing Burnout* (San Francisco, CA: Jossey-Bass, 2005), 2-3.

Chi Eng Yuan

narrative (Gen 2:2-3), celebrated in Psalms (Ps 8:3, 19:1).[10]

What happened after the fall?[11] While God set Adam to work in the Garden of Eden for his benefit, the fall introduced a dark aspect of work. Bruce Waltke points out that:

> The end result of total depravity is that without God's gracious Intervention, unregenerate people struggle to live between the demands of their conscience and their drives and appetites. They do everything with mixed motives, producing mixed results. Moreover, because of original sin and total depravity, humanity has built a culture which glorifies not God but self. Because of the Fall, their accomplishments at best are tarnished.[12]

As a result of the fall, Adam and later generations have had to wrest their living from the ground by "painful toil." (Gen. 3:17 NIV)[13]

---

[10] James K. Mead, "Labor," in *The New Interpreter's Dictionary of the Bible*, 5 vols., ed. K. D. Sakefeld, vol. 5, (Nashville, TN: Abingdon, 2009), 554.

[11] There are positive and negative approaches about work after the fall. Some are positive, such as Mead (ibid.) who states that "The bible presents a certain tension over the drudgery that accompanies much physical labor (Gen 3:17-19)." Others are more negative, such as Vawter, Von Rad, and Westermann.

[12] Bruce W. Waltke and Charles Yu, *An Old Testament Theology: An Exegetical, Canonical, and Thematic Approach* (Grand Rapids, MI: Zondervan, 2006), 280.

[13] See William H. U. Anderson, "The Curse of Work in Qoheleth: An Exposition of Genesis 3:17-19 in Ecclesiastes," *Evangelical Quarterly* 70, no. 2 (1998): 101-104. Anderson argues that Westermann, Vawter, and Von Rad would agree that "all human work in the world is racked with problems, frustration and pain. . . . [I]t is the implications of the curse which determined the extent and potency of it in life. And this is what Qoheleth focuses on: the all-pervasive effects of the curse in Gn. 3:17-19 in the activities of humans 'under the sun'."

This kind of emotional exhaustion is the root of burnout, as seen in the dark side of toil. Since the fall, work can be unpleasant and frustrating, plunging human beings into rounds of drudgery that never yield recognition, profit, or reward.[14] This word "work" is chosen by Solomon to describe the labor he invested in his pursuit of life's meaning apart from God. Solomon reported, "My heart took delight in all my work, and this was the reward for all my labor. Yet when I surveyed all that my hands had done and what I had toiled to achieve, everything was meaningless, a chase after the wind; nothing was gained under the sun." (Eccl. 2:10-11 NIV)

The most common biblical word that seems to be identified with burnout is "weary" or "worn out." *Yāgā'* means "to toil" or "to labor" but emphasizes the exhaustion that hard work entails.[15] The root meaning reflects "an emphasis on the toil of work and the weariness that results from labor."[16] Toil, in this context, exacts a cost disproportionate to the benefit received. The notion of "growing weary" reflects the process of emotional exhaustion. This is the word used when the Bible says: "Do not wear yourself out to get rich; have the wisdom to show restraint." (Prov. 23:4 NIV) The root meaning of "weary"—"be (become) tired"—gives rise to other connotations such as "be (or become) faint," "be (or become) powerless," and "be (or become) exhausted."[17] In the LXX (Greek OT), the terms "be exhausted" (Hab. 2:13 NIV) and "become tired" (Jer. 2:24 HCSB) are used as synonyms for "growing weary."[18] The sequence in 1 Kings

---

[14] Lawrence O. Richards, *Expository Dictionary of Biblical Words* (Grand Rapids, MI: Zondervan, 1985), 636.

[15] Ibid.

[16] Ralph H. Alexhander, "Toil, Labor, Grow, Be Weary," in *Theological Wordbook of the Old Testament*, vol. 1, ed. R. Laird Harris, Gleason Archer, and Bruce Waltke (Chicago: Moody, 1980), 362.

[17] G. F. Hasel, "yaga'," in *Theological Dictionary of the Old Testament*, vol. 6, ed. G. J. Botterweck, H. Ringgren, and H.-J. Fabry (Grand Rapids: Eerdmans, 1977), 151.

[18] Ibid., 152.

19—"hungry, weary, thirsty"—shows the reciprocal influence of body and soul to bring one to burnout.[19] However, God reassures his people that even though youths grow weary and faint, God never tires.

The verb *talaiporeō* describes those who suffer hardship, even to the point of physical or emotional exhaustion (Isa. 33:1; Jer. 4:13, 20: 10:20). In Isaiah 33:1 (LXX), *talaiporeō* means "to distress, make weary." Though the God of Israel hides his face in wrath, he returns to his people with everlasting grace (Isa. 45:15; 54:8). And though the people of Israel may feel that God does not see their plight, they are not cut off from the comfort of the Lord, who gives power and strength to the weary (Isa. 40:27, 29).[20]

The New Testament provides solid wisdom on how to deal with "burnout" or "weariness" (Matt. 11:28-30 NIV). Jesus, who alone reveals the Father and His divine plan of redemption, calls out: "Come to me, all you who are weary and burdened, and I will give you rest." Jesus called Peter and Andrew with a similar expression (4:19, lit. "Come after me"). "Come to me," is a tender call to intimacy with Him for all those who are weary and burdened. "Weary" evokes an image of people weighed down with heavy loads. But his yoke—a metaphor of discipleship—promises rest from the weariness and burden of religious regulations and human oppression. It is nothing other than commitment to follow him. His disciples learn directly from him. As the messianic inaugurator of the Kingdom of Heaven, Jesus offers rest in himself for their souls, in his authoritative understanding of God's truth. His yoke brings true learning about righteousness in the Sermon on the Mount where he declares that he has come to fulfill the Law. Jesus taught and displayed the righteousness that the Law was always meant to reflect (Matt. 5:17-48).

---

[19] Ibid., 153.

[20] Roland K. Harrison, "Talaiporeo," in *The New International Dictionary of New Testament Theology*, ed. Colin Brown, vol. 3 (Grand Rapids: Zondervan, 1979), 859.

The yoke of discipleship brings rest because Jesus is "gentle and humble in heart" (Matt. 11:29, NIV). Jesus exemplifies the very characteristics his disciples are to display as members of the Kingdom of Heaven—gentleness (Matt. 5:5) and humility (James 4:6; 1 Pet. 5:5).[21] This rest, a spiritual rest in Christ, through the Holy Spirit, does not exempt the disciples from hard work but provides the strength to overcome "a certain measure of fear, anxiety, uncertainty and meaninglessness."[22] Ironically, Jesus teaches his disciples, the pastors of the early churches, that while the disciple is to be "perfect" (Matt. 5:48 NIV), daily life and ministry can be experienced without burnout (11:28-30)! The disciples can rely, as Jesus did, on the help of the Holy Spirit for the guidance and power to fulfill the "deepest of the human longings."[23]

Jesus did not demand a "sinless perfection" but commanded us to reflect God's character in every aspect of our lives. William Klein explains that "perfect" means that "those who live in relationships of wholeness do not hate a brother and sister, do not seek to possess or use other people as objects, do honor their marriage commitments, do deal completely truthfully with all people, and rather than retaliate, they seek other people's—even their enemies'—best interests above their own."[24]

Doug Webster further illuminates the nature of Jesus' yoke:

> His easy yoke is neither cheap nor convenient. The surprising promise of the easy yoke was meant to free us from a self-serving, meritorious, performance-based religion. It is easy in that it frees us from the

---

[21] Michael J. Wilkins, *The NIV Application Commentary: Matthew* (Grand Rapids, MI: Zondervan, 2004), 422-24

[22] Craig L. Blomberg, *Matthew*, New American Commentary (Nashville, TN: Broadman, 1992), 194.

[23] Ibid., 192.

[24] William W. Klein, *Become What You Are* (Tyrone, GA: Authentic, 2006), 129.

burden of self-centeredness; liberates us from the load of self-righteousness; and frees us to live in the way that God intended us to live. . . . The easy yoke sounds like an oxymoron. Plowing a field or pulling a load is hard work! And nowhere does Jesus promise soft ground for tilling or level paths for bearing the load. What he does promise is a relationship with Him. The demands are great but our relationship with Jesus makes the burden light.[25]

Paul uses the same word (work/labor) in a special sense referring to work that labors for the Lord Jesus Christ. For Paul it was a labor of love (Rom. 16:12; 1 Cor. 16:16; 1 Thess. 1:3; 5:12).

Biblical Examples that May Reflect the Symptoms of Burnout

Moses

Moses was a faithful man of God, but he began to show evidence of burnout syndrome over many years as he coped with the demands of the Israelites. While not explicitly described as such in Scripture, Moses resembles a pastor who enters ministry to serve people but then comes to resent them. Numbers 11:4-6 NIV describes the Israelites' complaints to Moses: "The rabble with them began to crave other food, and again the Israelites started wailing and said, 'If only we had meat to eat! We remember the fish we ate in Egypt at no cost—also the cucumbers, melons, leeks, onions and garlic. But now we have lost our appetite; we never see anything but this manna!'"

The people complained bitterly about God's provision, directing their complaints to Moses. Later, "Moses heard the people of every family wailing, each at the entrance to his tent. The Lord became exceedingly angry, and Moses was troubled. He asked the Lord,

---

[25] Doug Webster, *Easy Yoke* (Colorado Springs, CO: NavPress, 1995), 8, 14.

'Why have you brought this trouble on your servant?' " (Num. 11:10-11 NIV) Moses turned the situation back over to God, describing himself as "weary": "I cannot carry all these people by myself; the burden is too heavy for me." (Num. 11:14 NIV)

Moses resented the Israelites and wanted to give up all responsibility. He faced his emotional exhaustion honestly and asked God to put him to death. A major problem for Moses was that he alone sat as judge and civil arbiter for all the people. He says, "The people come to me to seek God's will. Whenever they have a dispute, it is brought to me, and I decide between the parties and inform them of God's decrees and laws." (Exod. 18: 15-16 NIV) Moses overburdened himself because he did not seek qualified helpers or equip others to become team members. He did not delegate responsibility and became exhausted. Finally, Moses's father-in-law advised him to recruit others to lead the Israelites.

In *Wounded Saints* Fran Sciacca suggests that Moses' thinking harbored six fallacies:

Fallacy #1: "I don't have time to train someone to help."
Fallacy #2: "No one knows how to do this right except me."
Fallacy #3: "If I don't do it myself, it'll never get done."
Fallacy #4: "No one else has my dedication and commitment."
Fallacy #5: "The more productive I am, the better employee I am."
Fallacy #6: "It's my job."[26]

Moses was similar to Elijah in believing these fallacies. Both firmly believed they alone were left to serve God with total commitment (I Kings 17–19).

The Exodus narrative introduces Moses as a man chosen to lead the Israelites out of Egyptian bondage. He was the shepherd whom God sent; however, from the beginning, Moses exhibited one of the warning signs for burnout: a mindset of inferiority. He asked, "Who

---

[26] Fran Sciacca, *Wounded Saints* (Grand Rapids, MI: Baker, 1992), 69-75.

am I that I should go to Pharaoh and bring the sons of Israel out of Egypt?" (Exod. 3:11 NIV) That question reveals a radical change in Moses; 40 years earlier he impulsively vindicated a fellow Hebrew whom an Egyptian had beaten (Exod. 2:11-12 NIV). Later, he felt inadequate for the task, even though God Himself commissioned him to lead. God responded to Moses, "I will be with you. And this will be the sign to you that it is I who have sent you: When you have brought the people out of Egypt, you will worship God on this mountain." (Exod. 3:12 NIV)

Moses then asked, "What shall I tell them?" (Exod. 3:13 NIV), realizing that demanding the release of a huge slave population would be difficult. Moses needed an authority higher than himself to persuade Pharaoh, and God responded, "I AM WHO I AM. This is what you are to say to the Israelites: 'I AM has sent me to you.' " (Exod. 3:14 NIV) In calling Himself "I AM," God revealed His identity as the eternal God who is always there for His people (Exod. 3:15-17). Still unconvinced, Moses asked, "What if they do not believe me?" (Exod. 4:1 NIV) God told Moses that He would validate his leadership through a series of miracles that would convince the Egyptians. Moses' final objection implied that he did not feel qualified to lead the people to freedom because he was not an eloquent speaker (Exod. 4:10). God responded to Moses with compassion and promised to give him words to say and He provided a team member, Aaron, for support.

For Moses the promise of God's assistance did not result in immediate success. Pharaoh answered Moses' words with arrogance: "Who is the Lord, that I should heed his voice and let Israel go? I do not know the Lord and I will not let Israel go." (Exod. 5:2 NIV) Moses and Aaron continued to negotiate and proposed a three-day journey into the wilderness rather than a complete exodus. Pharaoh refused to free the people, even for a short period, and only increased the workload of the Hebrew slaves (Exod. 5:10-14).

The people "rewarded" Moses and Aaron's efforts to liberate them from slavery by naming them in a lawsuit (Exod. 5:20-21). The oppressed people turned on their liberators, and Moses and Aaron were charged with actions punishable by death. In despair, Moses responded to the people's rejection of his leadership by questioning God. He stated, "O Lord, why have you brought trouble upon this people? Is this why you sent me?" (Exod. 5:22 NIV) Moses' inability to stave off the people's rebellion in the wilderness drove him to a crisis of faith. He felt like a failure and accused God of failure (Exod. 5:3-22). Moses' feelings of rejection and failure resulted in symptoms of burnout: physical, emotional, mental, and spiritual exhaustion.

Elijah

First Kings narrates the story of the prophet Elijah and his burnout experience, which resembles that of contemporary pastors. When Elijah is introduced in 1 Kings 17:1 NIV, he is already in experiencing conflict: "Now Elijah the Tishbite, from Tishbe in Gilead, said to Ahab, 'As the Lord, the God of Israel, lives, whom I serve, there will be neither dew nor rain in the next few years except at my word.' " Elijah had been in Israel long enough to have earned the reputation as one who knew God intimately and walked with Him faithfully. He was a seasoned, experienced prophet of God who had witnessed many miracles, and his prayers had brought both a famine and the raising of a young boy from the dead.

The prophet Obadiah met Elijah in a field one day, and Elijah told him to ask King Ahab to come to Elijah. Obadiah panicked and asked, "What have I done wrong, that you are handing your servant over to Ahab to be put to death?" (1 Kings 18:9 NIV) For three years famine had plagued the land as a result of Elijah's prayers, and Ahab sought to kill Elijah. Obadiah told Elijah he feared that as soon as he went to get the king, Elijah would disappear and that, in his anger, Ahab would kill Obadiah (1 Kings 18:12).

Now Elijah was very important to God; he even appears in the New Testament. The last Old Testament prophet predicted

Elijah's return, and the New Testament begins with the appearance of John the Baptist, whom Jesus affirmed was the fulfillment of that prophecy (Luke 7:24-30). Elijah and Moses were both present at the transfiguration (Luke 9:29-33).

Even so, Elijah still experienced symptoms of burnout. He hid in the Judean countryside because Jezebel was furious after Ahab recounted for her the incident in which Elijah "had killed all the prophets of Baal with the sword" on Mount Carmel (1 Kings 19:1 NIV). After this experience, Elijah developed mental exhaustion and feelings of inferiority. Terrified of Jezebel's threats, Elijah "ran for his life" (1 Kings 19:3) and "prayed that he might die, and said, 'It is enough! Now, Lord, take my life, for I am no better than my ancestors.' " (1 Kings 19:4 NIV) This prayer for escape through death was evidence of burnout; his depression demonstrated several common symptoms of the syndrome.

Elijah suffered physical exhaustion after killing hundreds of false prophets on Mt. Carmel (1 Kings 18:16-14). Following this experience, Elijah fled the king's boundaries when Jezebel threatened him and felt too weak to continue. Even small challenges were difficult for the prophet in the face of his burnout, and Elijah could not believe that God would protect him from Jezebel. His emotional exhaustion surfaced as hopelessness: He collapsed under a tree and told God that life was hopeless and he wanted to die. He could not see God's hand and believed Jezebel would succeed in her plot to have his head. Elijah's emotional exhaustion was also evident when he told God, "I have been very zealous for the Lord God Almighty. The Israelites have rejected your covenant, broken down your altars, and put your prophets to death with the sword. I am the only one left, and now they are trying to kill me too" (1 Kings 19:10 NIV). This verse reveals Elijah's unrealistic expectations of himself and the people of Israel. He had high hopes of national repentance in Israel, but his expectations were not fulfilled. As Elijah's hope and expectations faded, and he became disillusioned and apathetic, which is one of the final stages of burnout. Physical, emotional, and mental exhaustion affected him psychologically and spiritually because he had not spent adequate time with God. Elijah's experience is typical of a man of God whose personal expectations exceed his resources. He is overcommitted and, rather than doing God's will, he relies on his own inadequate strength and determination to do God's work.

Jeremiah

Jeremiah's character has two sides. On one hand, he was very devoted to the Lord and boldly denounced Judah's sins with no positive feedback; on the other hand, he struggled with feelings of depression, doubt and despair. At the brink of exhaustion, he questioned the meaning of his ministry (Jer. 15:10-21) and challenged the Lord about whether His word would be fulfilled (Jer. 17:12-18). At the peak of his emotional distress, he cried out to the Lord, "You deceived me," (Jer. 20:7 NIV) and cursed the day of his birth (Jer. 20:14-18) because the response to his ministry totally failed to meet his expectations; he was repeatedly dismissed and had no sense of accomplishment. But one thing kept him from dropping out: He did not hesitate to express his genuine emotion to God.

Jeremiah suffered burnout symptoms, just like many contemporary pastors. He was consumed by zeal for the Lord and by his own zeal. He was eager to serve the Lord but, when he failed to get positive feedback from the people, Jeremiah reacted negatively: "Should good be repaid with evil? Yet they have dug a pit for me. Remember that I stood before you and spoke in their behalf to turn your wrath away from them. So give their children over to famine; hand them over to the power of the sword. Let their wives be made childless and widows; let their men be put to death, their young men slain by the sword in battle" (Jer. 18:20-21 NIV).

Jeremiah hoped that, after being confronted with God's word, his flock would respond. In her book *A Time for Healing*, Jody

Seymour summarizes the disillusionment that progressed to despair on Jeremiah's path to burnout:

> O Lord, you deceived me, and I was deceived, you overpowered me and prevailed. I am ridiculed all day long; everyone mocks me. Cursed be the day I was born! May the day my mother bore me not be blessed! Why did I ever come out of the womb to see trouble and sorrow and to end my days in shame? (Jer. 20:7, 14, 18 NIV)[27]

Seymour recognizes the spiritual dryness and smoldering bitterness evidenced by these sentiments as key symptoms of pastoral burnout:

> Those last words that Jeremiah used to describe the God who had called him should ring in the soul of many of us who are ordained. The journey of ministry gets long and sometimes very dry. We are supposed to be the ones who lead our flocks to green pastures beside the still waters. What happens when we feel like God has led us to a dried-up brook? What happens when we need some water to put out the slow-burning fire within us that is burning us out?[28]

Basic Definition of Burning Up/Passion/Zeal

"Human beings are born to burn for something, no matter whether it is real or false, true or untrue, right or wrong . . . coming from the desire that engraves the deep part of our souls."

---

[27] Jody Seymour, *A Time for Healing: Overcoming the Perils of Ministry* (Valley Forge, PA: Judson, 1995), 32-33.
[28] Ibid., 34.

I recently read this definition in our church newsletter: "Passion is the heart set free to pursue that which is truly worthy. Those who set their hearts on what is most worthy—The Glory of God—live with joy-filled abandon. Their hearts are both seized and satisfied with ambition for Jesus to be ardently worshiped. That love comes to dominate and integrate all other desires so that they live in the freedom of single-minded purpose." —*Bethany Evangelical Free Church Newsletter*

"Zeal" describes God's fervor (Isa 9:7; 26:11; 37:32) as well as human passion for God's righteousness (Ps 119:139). In the Old Testament, by zealously killing a brazen offender, Phinehas (grandson of Aaron, a priest) appeases Yahweh's anger (Num 25:11). Numbers 25 says that the zeal of Phineas for Yahweh has turned away the anger of Yahweh and protected Israel from destruction (Num 25:11-13). Honor goes to Phinehas because he is zealous for the Lord with God's zeal, so that the Lord in his zeal does not wipe out the Israelites. Phinehas, a man of godly passion and knowledge, but not self-motivated zeal, is promised the covenant of a lasting priesthood "because he was zealous for the honor of his God" (Num. 25:13, NIV). Psalm 106:31, NIV adds the idea that Phinehas's intervention "was credited to him as righteousness for endless generations to come." This echoes the commendation of Abraham when he believed the Lord (Gen 15:6).

Elijah was "zealous for the Lord" when he executed the prophets of Baal, then fled for his life (I Kings 18:40; 19:10 DRA). Elijah's zeal for the cause of Yahweh resulted in unqualified devotion and passion against the forces of Ahab and Baalism (19:10, 14). The wording in both statements involves an infinitive absolute, a grammatical stratagem that bespeaks enormous intensity. It is evident that, in this zeal, as often happens to the zealous, Elijah has overvalued his own significance. Nevertheless, the final utterance of Yahweh checks Elijah's (self-serving?) zeal. In fact, it is not true that "I,

I only am left." In truth there are 7,000 uncompromised, 7,000 unacknowledged by Elijah. His sense of his own importance has blinded him to the political shape of the conflict. There are allies he has not noticed.

In Ezekiel 36:5a NIV, "this is what the Sovereign Lord says: In my burning zeal I have spoken against the rest of the nations, and against all Edom." Jesus cleansing the Temple stirs in his disciples the memory of Jesus as *righteous sufferer* (Ps 69:9). Although God's people were warned against "zeal without knowledge" (Prov. 19:2, NIV, cf. Rom.10:2), religious zeal was an important part of Jewish piety. In fact, God himself is shown to be zealous for his holy name (Isa. 59:17; Ezek. 39:25).

In the New Testament, Jesus's zeal, righteous rather than blindly nationalistic, was so great that it would "consume" him. This refers to his death, which would bring life to the world. As we read in Luke 24:32 NIV, the disciples asked each other, "Were not our hearts burning within us while he talked with us on the road and opened the Scriptures to us?" Howard Marshall pointed out "the story may be then suggesting that, in the light of the disciples' experience, later believers may be able to recognize their inward warmth of heart as springing from the presence of the risen Lord.

"A foretaste of Pentecostal fire, burning high and long . . . we learn that not only were their minds informed, but their hearts were also touched. Perhaps now they would be ready for faith in the scriptural witness to the destiny of Jesus as the Christ." [29]

Paul also describes himself as once having been so zealous in his devotion to the Lord that he persecuted the church (Acts 22:3-4; Gal 1:13 14; Phil 3:6), and rejoices in the zeal expressed by the repentant Corinthians (2 Cor. 7:7-12).

In one of Paul's letters, (Rom. 12:2) "zeal" emerged as an especially commendable characteristic in the intertestamental

---

[29] Howard Marshall, *The Gospel of Luke* (Grand Rapids, Michigan:Eerdmans, 1979), 899.

period, when the very existence of the Jewish faith was threatened by foreign enemies and internal unconcern. It is also uniformly praised in the NT. Paul's "testimony" about Israel begins, then, on a positive note: They have a praiseworthy devotion to God. The problem with Israel and the reason Paul must continue to pray for its salvation is that, like pre-Christian Paul, the Israelites' zeal is not driven by "knowledge"—specifically, practical/applied, rather than merely theoretical, experiential knowledge of God that would have resulted in glorifying and thanking Him. From Romans 12:11 NIV: "Never be lacking in zeal, but keep your spiritual fervor, serving the Lord."

In his call for us to love and esteem one another in v.10, Paul warns about laziness in zeal. "In brotherly love, be heartfelt in your love to one another. Honor one another above yourselves. Never be lacking in zeal, but keep your spiritual fervor, serving the Lord." (Rom. 12:11 NIV) The temptation to "lose steam" in our lifelong responsibility to pursue reverently what is "good, well pleasing to God, and perfect," is a natural one —but it must be strenuously resisted.

The idea of "zeal" (to boil, seethe) is continued in the image of "being set on fire" (as Appollo's "fervent in spirit" Acts 18:25 ASV) in the second exhortation. Paul is exhorting us to call the Holy Spirit to "set us on fire" ("by the Spirit"), to open ourselves to the Spirit as he seeks to excite us about the "rational worship" to which the Lord has called us. But "set us on fire" is open to abuse, so Paul preempted any such abuse by reminding us that being set on fire by the Holy Spirit must lead to, and be directed by, our service to the Lord. We cannot be so carried away by enthusiasm for spiritual things that we leave behind the objective standards of Christian living that the Scriptures set forth. This enthusiasm is not a kind of self-centered display (such as characterized the Corinthians) but the enthusiasm of humble service to the Master.[30]

---

[30] Douglas J. Moo, *The Epistle to the Romans*(Grand Rapids, Michigan:Eerdmans, 1996), 778-9.

Six causes of burnout that matter

Spirituality matters

Pastors, church planners and missionaries are invariably at risk of spiritual *dryness*. Seeking life from sources other than God (Jeremiah 2:13) or Jesus Christ can be devastating to those called out of the "desert" to the "living water . . . welling up to eternal life" (John 4:10, 14 NIV). Jeremiah described such "spiritual dryness" in someone who is avoiding God, saying that he will be "like a bush in the wastelands; he will not see prosperity when it comes. He will dwell in the parched places of the desert, in a salt land where no one lives" (Jeremiah 17:6 NIV).

Spiritual dryness occurs when a pastor feels he has no time for, or spends less time in, devotions, being alone with God. The result is a minister who begins to feel like a plant without water. Comparing similar patterns throughout the course of church history, theologians such as Bruce Demarest and Charles Raup (in their article for *Criswell Theological Review*, "Recovering the Heart of Christian Spirituality") warn that American Christianity suffers from excessive dependence on a "self-determination," "intellectualism," and "ethical achievements."

Rest matters

Survey after survey has documented the role of insufficient rest in burnout among clergy. Excessive demands on time—fueled by unrealistic expectations placed on pastors by both their congregations and themselves—and the attendant lack of sufficient rest have become the norm among pastors nowadays.

Burnout occurs not only because of a heavy workload, but also because of not taking adequate time for Sabbath and rest. The association of Sabbath with creation, found in Genesis 2:1-3 and Exodus 20:11, is part of the fourth commandment. Under normal circumstances a day other than Sunday is usually set aside for pastors to spend time with God, family, and others. That day is the *Pastor's* Sabbath. By understanding the true meaning of the Sabbath, any time or day can become a Pastor's Sabbath, because the same Resurrection that inaugurated our Lord's present reign in power and attested to His deity has also transformed every day into His day.

Compatibility matters

Incompatibility with ministry may occur when an individual does not appreciate the true nature of the pastorate or the extent of his own personal limitations and gifts. When pastors believe themselves to be inferior and incapable of facing the challenges, it is typically because (1) they have doubts about their callings; (2) the particular pastoral position comes with an overwhelming job description; and (3) lay leaders and congregations reinforce the natural tendency to put pastors on pedestals.

That is the time for the pastor to review God's calling, for God is the one who provides the strength for His servants to meet the needs of the sheep, and He never leaves a pastor without the resources needed to fulfill his calling. The pastor also needs to wrestle with Jesus's call for His disciples to be "servants of the Lord"; spiritual authority and leadership come only through the path of suffering and sacrifice (Mark 10:38-39). For example, Paul did not abuse his leadership position but was humble enough to serve with those same status symbols (2 Corinthians 3:9; 11:26-29).

Confidant matters

A Christian minister needs a support system when it's necessary to reestablish priorities, regain perspective, and find refuge in times of trouble. To find real friendship can be complicated, depending upon how the pastor views himself. If he views himself only in the terms of his vocation, a relational distance may separate him from the congregation. Finding the needed support is also compromised by a prevailing culture that promotes the values of individualism, intelligence and self-sacrifice.

There are times when the need for a confidant in ministry is imperative. Even Our Lord needed a personal confidant, a trustworthy disciple to support him. Jesus asked his disciples, especially his core group—Peter, James and John—to accompany Him when He prayed in the Garden of Gethsemane (Matthew 26:36-38). Paul, too, needed a confidant. He described Timothy as "one soul, one spirit, and one mind" with him, to share friendship (Philippians 1:27, 2:2 NIV). Thus, Paul naturally requested Timothy to be with him near the end of his life (2 Timothy 1:16-18; 4:17). He also treasured those "true yokefellows,… for they have labored side by side with me in the gospel" (Philippians 4:3 RSV). In his friendship with the church of Philippi, he was bathed in spiritual prayer and material support.

Conflict matters

Conflict is another significant factor that may contribute to burnout. My research shows that it is not uncommon for a pastor to be forced out as a direct result of conflict between himself and powerful leaders, or between a senior pastor and other pastoral staff. Since conflict in ministry is inevitable, and unresolved conflict likely contributes to burnout, it is critical for a pastor to manage conflict effectively, both with other pastoral staff and with the congregation.

While conflict can display the true character of a pastor, it can also push a pastor into imbalance, and even progress to burnout. Paul's experience recorded in 2 Corinthians made him the perfect candidate for burnout. He loved the Corinthian church but encountered repeated challenges and even attacks from the

Corinthian congregation. He was at great risk of emotional exhaustion and withdrawal from those who attacked him, and it could well have caused him to evaluate himself negatively, particularly in regard to his ministry with the Corinthians. Tension between a godly pastor and a worldly church, resulting in emotional exhaustion or even burnout, can be due to longstanding conflict, just as in the church of Corinth in the first century.

Culture Matters

Cultural clash results from conflicting expectations between pastors and their congregations, or unrealistic expectations pastors might have of themselves. An individual may be exposed to multiple cultures from childhood, and these may clash significantly. Accepting a pastoral calling but failing to recognize the diverse cultural values one has absorbed may negatively impact one's ability to fulfill the pastoral role. Trying to meet all the various expectations associated with one's family, national and racial values may create tension, anxiety, weariness and depression, all of which contribute to burnout.

Christian ministers should present their whole lives to God as a sacrifice (Romans 12:1). However, when cultures do clash, similarities and differences must be addressed to avoid confusion and conflict. Even when we belong to a new realm—a new culture from the Lord Jesus Christ—we must still resist the influence of the old realm. That is why Paul commanded us "not to be conformed to this world" but "be transformed by the renewing of your mind," a lifelong process of "approving the will of God," as pastors understand, agree with, and put into practice God's will by following the Holy Spirit (Romans 12:2 NIV).

A complete approach places all the relationships of a Christian minister's life in a cross shape that includes one's vertical relationship with God and self, and a horizontal relationship with others and with culture.

This book consists of two major sections. In the first major section, Chapters 2 through 4 are about our vertical relationship with God in terms of our passion to serve, our spirituality, our understanding and practice of *rest* (Sabbath), and our compatibility. In the second major section, Chapters 5 through 7 are about our horizontal relationship with others in terms of our confidant, our management of conflict with others and our approach to the culture around us. As we walk the steps of this journey, please remember to take up the cross (vertical *and* horizontal) for the one who calls us, and we will see the crown from Heaven. For, as Apostle Peter later wrote: "Care for the flock that God has entrusted to you. Watch over it willingly, not grudgingly—not for what you will get out of it, but because you are eager to serve God. Don't lord it over the people assigned to your care, but lead them by your good example. And when the Great Shepherd appears, you will receive a crown of glory and honor." (1 Peter 5:2-4 NLT.)

At one time or another, all ministers ask the questions or face the challenges of losing their passion for ministry. This author contends that the major contributor to a loss of passion or interest in ministry in general is *burnout*. The following chapters will survey the causes of burnout and will end with suggested methods of overcoming it.

2

Christ-centered spirituality: From Spiritual Dryness to Spiritual Fruitfulness

The reality of Spiritual Dryness

What is spirituality? "Spirituality" is a term used to describe those who are under the influence of the Holy Spirit.[31] In common usage, spirituality has come to refer to a variety of different religious experiences, but in this book the meaning is limited to describing *Christian* spirituality, which "must be biblical in the sense that it flows from, incarnates, is normed by, and rests upon the authority of Scripture for its claim to be a genuine response to the initiative of God in revelation."[32]

There are biblical analogies for spiritual dryness. We read in William L. Holladay's *Jeremiah 1: a Commentary on the Book of the Prophet Jeremiah Chapters 1-25* that God is "depicted metaphorically

---

[31] Sandra M. Schneiders, "Spirituality," in *The New Interpreter's Dictionary of the Bible*, vol. 5, ed. K. D. Sakefeld, (Nashville, TN: Abingdon, 2009), 365.
[32] Ibid., 367.

as a 'spring of running water.' "[33] This reveals two aspects of Jeremiah's indictment against Israel, God's chosen people, who reject God as the source of life as they replace Him with earthly support systems which are no more than "cracked and leaky cisterns."[34] Jeremiah's subsequent description of one who turns away from God reflects the very essence of the term "spiritual dryness": he "will be like a bush in the wastelands; he will not see prosperity when it comes. He will dwell in the parched places of the desert, in a salt land where no one lives." (Jeremiah. 17:6,NIV)

The Old Testament theme of God as a "spring of running water" translates into "streams of living water" in the New Testament, through Jesus Christ. Dr. Craig Blomberg, professor of *New Testament* at Denver Seminary, acknowledges that the metaphor of spiritual "living water" (John 4:10) finds "ample Old Testament precedent." (Ps. 36:9; Prov. 13:14; 18:4; 55:1; Ezek. 47:1-12; Zech.14:8)[35] Disciples are called from the "desert" to accept Jesus' offer of "living water . . . welling up to eternal life." (John 4:10, 14.) Without Christ's sustaining strength, the disciples can do nothing (John 15:5). Moreover, the OT notion of "Yahweh-alone"[36] is reflected in Jesus as the only "way." (John 14:6.) To reject Jesus is to reject the one who gives disciples, including pastors, new life and enables them to bear fruit. Similarly, in Psalm 1:3, "Fruit and foliage balance each other: Fruit is what the tree lives for, but without foliage there will be no fruit."[37]

Webster adds that "in biblical and Jewish tradition, 'living water' is salvific. Ezekiel 47 speaks of the rivers that arise from the temple

---

[33] William L. Holladay, *Jeremiah 1: A Commentary on the Book of the Prophet Jeremiah Chapters 1-25* (Philadelphia, PA: Fortress, 1984), 92.

[34] Page H. Kelley, Joel F. Drinkard, Jr., and Peter C. Craigie, *Jeremiah 1-25*, Word Biblical Commentary, vol. 26 (Dallas, TX: Word, 1991), 30.

[35] Craig L. Blomberg, *The Historical Reliability of John's Gospel* (Downers Grove, IL: InterVarsity, 2001), 100.

[36] Robert P. Carroll, *Jeremiah* (Philadelphia, PA: Westminster, 1986), 126.

[37] John Goldingay, *Psalms 1-41*, vol. 1 (Grand Rapids, MI: Baker, 2006), 85.

precinct and flow out to all nations, nourishing trees which 'bear fruit every month' and with healing in their leaves." (Ezek. 47:12.[38]) In other words, without intimacy with God, spiritual growth will be minimal or fail altogether, and the ministry may be unable to survive. Eugene Peterson, professor of spiritual theology at Regent College, further observes that:

> Jeremiah uses organic images for ways of life that either prevent or invite access to God, and in this he is in the biblical mainstream. A shrub in the desert and a tree by the river are both alive, but not quite in the same way: the desert shrub meagerly survives, the watered tree abundantly reproduces. The shrub in the desert is a cursed way of life, for it is only responsive to what is human ("trust in man"), and in itself a very minuscule portion of reality. The tree by the river is a blessed way of life, for it is responsive to what is divine ("whose trust is in the Lord"), and therefore open to the extravaganza of creation and redemption.[39]

Throughout the history of Christianity, churches have faced crises of spirituality. J. I. Packer, also a professor of theology at Regent College, warns of a trend in American Christianity that is "man-centered, manipulative, success-oriented, self-indulgent and sentimental . . . 3,000 miles wide and half an inch deep."[40] Ben Campbell Johnson, professor of Evangelism, Columbia Theological Seminary, also discusses the tendency toward legalism and a lack of the presence and guidance of the Holy Spirit in "conservative

---

[38] Jane S. Webster, *Ingesting Jesus: Eating and Drinking in the Gospel of John* (Atlanta, GA: Society of Biblical Literature, 2003), 55.
[39] Eugene H. Peterson, *Subversive Spirituality* (Grand Rapids, MI: Eerdmans, 1997), 82.
[40] J. I. Packer, *A Quest for Godliness* (Wheaton, IL: Crossway, 1990), 22.

churches with a puritan or revivalist tradition."[41] Bruce Demarest and Charles Raup, former professors at Denver Seminary, also echo this trend of ministers too busy for an intimate relationship with God, who rely on their own resources and talents more than the "living water." Some pursue intellectual excellence, others worldly success, at the expense of intimacy with God:

> Protestantism suffers from the scourge of intellectualism when it believes that deepest human needs can be satisfied by right thinking about God… Christendom furthermore suffers the scourge of moralism when it believes that ethical achievements, apart from a vital relationship with God, constitute the heart of the Christian life… Conceptual knowledge of God and good works must be joined with an experiential knowledge of God nurtured in an atmosphere of faith and commitment.[42]

Ministers are at risk of following the same path to "spiritual dryness" that is rampant in the Bible and throughout church history. Burnout is a prevalent spiritual disease among ministers who are "broken cisterns," for whom "intimacy with God has gone cold."[43]

Before 2004 few studies related burnout to the spirituality of pastors, but in 2004 Jonathan Golden and colleagues used the MBI-General Survey to assess burnout among clergy. They found that "although personality and situational factors were found to play important roles, spirituality, and especially that quality of spirituality

---

[41] Ben Cambell Johnson, *Pastoral Spirituality* (Philadelphia, PA: Westminster, 1988), 68-9.
[42] Bruce Demarest and Charles Raup, "Recovering the Heart of Christian Spirituality," *Criswell Theological Review* 3, no. 2 (1989): 322.
[43] Michael Todd Wilson and Brad Hoffmann, *Preventing Ministry Failure* (Downers Grove, IL: InterVarsity Press, 2007), 41.

which relates the individual to God through prayer or meditation, was also shown to be an important additional component in burnout."[44] It seemed that the condition of the pastors' spirituality actually did influence the appearance of burnout. A survey done by this author in 2006 and 2007 in a previous study of pastors' burnout revealed that spiritual dryness is a key factor in developing burnout symptoms. Spiritual dryness describes a condition in which the individual feels as if his or her worldly routine leaves too little or no time at all to spend with God in devotion and meditation.

Charles Caleb Colton, an English writer of the early 19th Century, observes the following about pastors' spiritual lives:

> He that studies only men, will get the body of knowledge without the soul; and he that studies only books, the soul without the body. He who adds observation to what he reads, reflection, is on the right road to knowledge, provided that in scrutinizing the hearts of others, he neglects not his own.[45]

In 2010 Dr. Diane J. Chandler, associate professor of Spiritual Formation and Leadership at Regent University, reported that average pastors work between 50 and 60 hours per week, spending little time with God and/or neglecting their own spiritual growth.[46] When pastors lose or fail to take time for prayer and meditation on God's Word, they may lose their grip on faith, lose joy in ministry and

---

[44] Jonathan Golden et al., "Spirituality and Burnout: An Incremental Validity Study," *Journal of Psychology & Theology* 32, no. 2 (Summer 2004):124.

[45] Caleb Colton, quoted in Richard Foster, *Celebration of Discipline: The Path to Spiritual Growth* (San Francisco: Harper & Row, 1988), 62 (emphasis added).

[46] Diane J. Chandler, "The Impact of Pastors' Spiritual Practices on Burnout," *The Journal of Pastoral Care & Counseling* 64, no. 2 (article 6) (2010): 1.

intimacy with God, and become increasingly judgmental.[47] Failure to maintain a consistent, disciplined spiritual life puts pastors on a path toward burnout, which can lead to further spiritual dryness and loss of intimacy with Christ, who alone can provide the energy to enable a God-directed ministry. Life in general can become shallow, and spiritual life may feel like a desert.

Howard Baker, instructor of Christian Formation at Denver Seminary, reflects on the spiritual toll that a demanding work week takes on the average pastor, quoting Jesus's words: "Are you tired? Worn out? Burned out on religion?"[48] Baker's spiritual dryness forced him to check the state of his inner life, which was being neglected and lacked spiritual discipline. He felt his soul had shrunk from a life of excessive work. He believed he lost his commitment because his own ambitions, rather than love for God, were the driving force in his life, and warns that this is an ongoing temptation for every pastor: "Pride—that old, original, and hidden sin—had directed me away from serving God into serving an image of myself buried deep under layers of religious work."[49] Pastors may seek refuge in the self and ignore the real needs of the soul. When they lie to themselves about their relationship with God, it affects the other aspects of their lives.

This author's previous survey reveals that, for some pastors, the taste of spiritual dryness is a useful wake-up call. For others, the lack of emotional and spiritual health can push a pastor into mental exhaustion, a clear symptom of burnout.[50] It may well be triggered when the pastor fails to fill the pews. The pastor of New Life Fellowship in Queens, N.Y., recalls experiencing this crisis:

---

[47] Lloyd Rediger, *Coping with Clergy Burnout* (Valley Forge, PA: Judson, 1982), 49.

[48] Howard Baker, *Soul Keeping* (Colorado Springs, CO: NavPress, 1998), 33, quoting Matt. 11:28a from *The Message* version of the Bible.

[49] Ibid., 35.

[50] Ibid.

"Pete, I'm leaving the church," my wife Geri had muttered quietly. I sat still, too stunned to respond.

"I can't take any more of this stress," she continued, "the constant crisis."

Geri had been more than patient. I had brought home constant pressure and tension from church, year after year. Now the woman I had promised to love as Christ loved the church was exhausted. We had experienced eight unrelenting years of stress.

"I'm not doing it anymore," she concluded. "This church is no longer life for me. It is death."

When a church member says, "I'm leaving the church," most pastors don't feel very good. But when your wife of nine years says it, your world is turned upside down. We were in the bedroom. I remember the day well.

"Pete, I love you, but I'm leaving the church," she summarized very calmly. "I no longer respect your leadership."

I was visibly shaken and didn't know what to say or do. I felt shamed, alone and angry.

I tried raising my voice to intimidate her: "That is out of the question," I bellowed. "All right, so I've made a few mistakes."

But she continued calmly. "It's not that simple. You don't have the guts to lead—to confront the people who need to be confronted. You don't lead. You're too afraid that people will leave the church. You're too afraid of what they'll think about you."

I was outraged.

"I'm getting to it!" I yelled defensively. "I'm working on it" (For the last two years, I really had been trying, but somehow still wasn't up to it.)

"Good for you, but I can't wait any more," she replied.[51]

This story parallels those of many other pastors.[52] Some find their lives are filled with meetings and fellowship, but they have no time for their families or God. The kind of commitment required to fulfill unrealistic expectations reduces a pastor's time and inclination to engage in critical self-examination. Under this strain pastors can suffer emotional, physical, behavioral and spiritual problems.

Ministers who are not deeply involved in God's Word are not sin-sensitive or healthy enough to break through layers of self-justification. Dr. Gordon McDonald, chancellor of Denver Seminary, discusses the danger of spiritual dryness, noting that it may be a leading cause of many pastors succumbing to dropout syndrome or, as he calls it: "DNF—Did Not Finish."[53] Additionally, Gary McIntosh, professor of Christian Ministry and Leadership at Fuller Seminary and Samuel D. Rima, the director of the Doctor of Ministry program at Bethel Seminary, explore this dark side of pastors' spiritual lives:

---

[51] Peter Scazzero and Warren Bird, *The Emotionally Healthy Church* (Grand Rapids, MI: Zondervan, 2003), 21.

[52] Yuan, responses to "4-Out" Questionnaire (November, 2006).

[53] Gordon McDonald, "Many in Leadership Did Not Finish: What Can We Do about That?" *Leadership Journal* 27, no. 1 (Winter 2006): 50.

If not tended, the mixture will ultimately explode with great ferocity. For some, the lid can be kept on for quite a period of time before the explosion finally occurs. Others sense the strange stirring and ominous bubbling deep inside, and not knowing for certain what is taking place, they periodically release a little of the pressure by lifting the lid in a solitary act of frustration or some other form of emotional release. Yet for others, those foreign stirrings deep within are denied, ignored, explained away.

. . . [They] explode in a sudden and massive moral failure or some other unexpected, shocking, or bizarre behavior. This denial and repression along with the resulting emotional explosion are particularly common among religious leaders who feel the constant need to be in total control of their lives so they can minister effectively to others. Regardless of how sudden the explosion may seem, it has been in the making since childhood.[54]

Pastors who do not intentionally put together and implement a spiritual growth plan set themselves up for a painful, inevitable experience. If they do not explore the "shadow" side of their spiritual leadership they will collapse into one of four syndromes: burnout, move out, dropout, or forced out.[55] Furthermore, pastors who do not focus on spiritual growth can experience moral misconduct and seem powerless to control dark compulsions such as indulging in pornography or a sexual affair.[56] They live in a self-made hell where moments of lustful pleasure are followed by hours of shame or even

---

[54] Gary L. McIntosh and Samuel D. Rima, *Overcoming the Dark Side of Leadership* (Grand Rapids, MI: Baker, 1997), 23.

[55] Yuan, responses to "4-Out" Questionnaire (November, 2006).

[56] Richard Exley, *Perils of Power* (Tulsa: Harrison House, 1988), 16-17.

days and weeks of unspeakable regret.[57] Until these pastors replace human lust with the desire for righteousness in daily intimacy with God ("walking in the light"), they will not enjoy their freedom in Christ and will continue to spiral down into spiritual decay.[58]

Indeed, in a survey on clergy who completed the MBI and other assessment tools, Benjamin Doolittle reported, "those who scored high on the spirituality scale also scored high on the personal accomplishment scale."[59] Douglas Turton and Leslie Francis reported, "a positive attitude toward prayer was associated with lower levels of emotional exhaustion, lower levels of depersonalization, and higher levels of a growing understanding of the psychological role of prayer in human functioning."[60]

In order to cope with the spiritual dryness of the pastors, the author suggests a journey "from Spiritual Dryness to Spiritual Fullness."

Journey to become Spiritually Fruitful

"Search me, O God, and know my heart; test me and know my anxious thoughts. See if there is any offensive way in me, and lead me in the way everlasting." (Psalm 139:23, 24, NIV)

"What a wretched man I am! Who will rescue me from this body of death? Thanks be to God—through Jesus Christ our Lord!" (Romans 7:24 NIV)

"Put on the full armor of God so that you can take your stand against the devil's schemes. For our struggle is not against flesh and blood, but against the rulers, against the authorities, against the

---

[57] Ibid.

[58] Yuan, responses to "4-Out" Questionnaire (November, 2006).

[59] Cited in Douglas W. Turton, Leslie J. Francis, and Christopher Alan Lewis, "Clergy Work-related Psychological Health, Stress, and Burnout," *Mental Health, Religion & Culture* 10, no. 1 (Jan 2007): 5.

[60] Ibid., 5.

powers of this dark world and against the spiritual forces of evil in the heavenly realms."(Ephesians 6:11-12 NIV)

True conversion brings true transformation. Conversion is the point at which we become a Christian, a process in which we cope with our flesh, our sinful nature and our dark side. Tim Addington, a former senior vice president with the Evangelical Free Church of America, notes that the dark side includes those areas where we are vulnerable to temptation, places of unresolved emotional issues that spill out to hurt others, uncontrolled anger, selfishness that leads to narcissism, poor treatment of those we lead, or other issues that cause upheaval spiritually, emotionally or relationally. Without soul-searching the depth of our spiritual life and without full awareness that a Christian minister's life is a day-by-day process of spiritual battles, victory in Christ will not be a reality. On the other hand, going deep and cleaning the "dust and dirt" from our relationship with God will bring new freshness and vital life in Christ. The spiritual "X-Ray" exam starts with questioning our relationship with God in terms of quality, quantity and purity.

The quality of a relationship with God reveals our knowing about God and our experience with God. It starts with our daily devotional time: prayer and the 3Ms of God's Word (Memorize, Meditate and Marinate), experiencing His presence, and full obedience to what God is teaching us.

While Christian ministers would not deny the importance of prayer, in their daily private lives prayer time with God in confession, petition, thanksgiving and adoration may actually be given a lower priority to other activities.

"The sacrifices of God are a broken spirit; a broken and contrite heart, O God, you will not despise." (Ps 51:17 NIV) Life is not *just* a journey. It is also a battleground for the struggle between the opposite poles of disgracing God and honoring Him. It is a time for continual healing of wounds, and for praying and planning a better strategy for victory for another day.

Confession is not a once-in-a-lifetime experience, but rather daily cleaning out the "closets" of our lives and keeping them clean.

As Christian ministers, we are "wretched." Repentance begins with admitting the sinful, vulnerable dark places in our lives. Our sins can cause us extreme shame, pain and guilt when we repeatedly view our failure. In order to stop the habit of sins, we must break through the dishonesty cycle—from openly lying, to the fear of discovery that causes us to cover up our sins by being less than honest. We can break this cycle by acknowledging the sins in our different "closets" without any excuses, totally trusting in God's forgiveness and healing. In my own experience, as I have repented from sin in one area, another is revealed and, as I repent of the sin in that area, yet more sinful territory is revealed. Even though these steps to recovery are painful, nailing my sins daily to the Cross is of great value in the eyes of our Lord.

Guide for Deep Cleaning of our Sins:

- Be aware that every temptation always starts from a naive or innocent move/half-truth/half-step;
- Be aware of the area where you are most vulnerable;
- Be aware of any hidden thoughts or issues because they represent the most dangerous parts of behavior patterns;
- Be aware of any process of hiding that leads to a way of wrong thinking; continue to maintain spiritual discernment through knowing God, yourself and others;
- Always be mindful of the internal process of "compartmentalization" between desire, thought and deed, the sinkhole for our dark-side which "steals and destroys" us;
- Be aware that the danger is not from the activity itself but our inclination toward self-deception. We must always check our hearts to see *why* and *how* it happened.

The temptation toward self-serving, self-interested prayers of petition is another area to which Christian minsters must pay attention. It is also tempting to reduce our private prayer life when we are also praying publicly. Simon Chan, professor of Systematic Theology at Trinity Theological College, Singapore, points out that we attempt to make prayer work for us rather than seeking God's sovereignty.[61] To cope with impurity in the act of prayer for those who serve the One who teaches us the Lord's Prayer, Simon suggests we move from self-centered prayers of petition to God-directed prayers of adoration and thanksgiving.[62]

George Muller, founder of Christian orphanages in Bristol, England, was a diligent Christian minister with a passion to pray. When Muller prayed, he was "communicating with Someone who genuinely was listening."[63] He also established a discipline of prayer, spending considerable time with the Lord, deepening his understanding of God's will and purifying his motives to desire God's agenda only. He wrote, "I seek the will of the Spirit of God through, or in connection with, the Word of God. The Spirit and the Word must be combined. If I look to the Spirit alone without the Word, I lay myself open to great delusions also. If the Holy Spirit guides us at all, He will do it according to the Scriptures and never contrary to them. Next I take into account providential circumstances. There often plainly indicate God's will in connection with His Word and Spirit. I ask God in prayer to reveal His will to me aright. Thus through praying to God, the study of the Word, and reflection, I come to a decision according to the best of my ability and knowledge; and if my mind is thus at peace, and continues so after two or three more petitions, I proceed accordingly. In both trivial matters, and in transactions involving very important issues, I have found this method effective."[64] Through his years of ministry,

---

[61] Simon Chan, *Spiritual Theology* (Downers Grove, IL, InterVarsity, 1998), 131.

[62] Ibid., 132.

[63] Kevin J Navarro, *The Spiritual Disciplines of George Muller* (homework assignment for class with Dallas Willard, 1993), 18.

[64] Ibid., 20.

Muller prayed, worked, made decisions and watched the Lord of the Universe answering his prayers in His time and in His way.[65]

It is dangerous when Christian ministers spend insufficient time and depth in quality, quantity and purity of studying and knowing God's Word. A spiritual X-ray asks the question: "Has my devotional time become a means to an end, such as preparing a sermon and/ or a Bible study, rather than spending time with God and hearing His Voice?"

In addition, memorizing Scripture makes a big difference in our ability to make good use of the "sword of the Spirit" (Ephesians 6:17b NIV). The habit of memorizing Bible passages is a "must" to re-connect with God and his protection of us, as seen in Psalms 119:11 NIV: "I have hidden your word in my heart that I might not sin against you." Even Jesus Christ was victorious in all the temptations of his life through his deep knowledge of God's Word (Luke 4:1-13 NIV). It is wise to both read and write out scriptural passages to be memorized, and to place them where they will be noticed and reviewed on a daily basis. And, of course, at the bottom lies a burning heart and a passion to memorize God's Word.

God commands Joshua to meditate on His Word: "Study this Book of Instruction continually. Meditate on it day and night so you will be sure to obey everything written in it. Only then will you prosper and succeed in all you do" (Joshua 1:8 NLT) After I became a Christian at the age of eight, I was delighted with the words "on his law he meditates day and night." (Psalm 1:2 NIV)

Lectio Divina is one of the best ways to mediate upon God's Word. Its four steps include:

- *Lectio* - Read the passage for it's content and meaning;
- *Meditatio* - Read again, this time noting a word or phrase that impresses or captures you;

---

[65] Ibid., 33.

- *Oratio* - Read again, this time taking the word or phrase to God in prayer, listening for what He unpacks for you around it, and;
- *Contempato* - Read again, this time just resting in God's presence and/or centering prayer.

George Muller was not only a Christian minister of prayer but also a man on fire to study God's Word. He went deeper and became closer to God through meditation on the Word of God:

"The most important thing I had to do was to read the Word of God and to meditate on it. ... It often astonishes me that I did not see the importance of meditation upon Scripture earlier in my Christian life. As the outward man is not fit for work for any length of time unless he eats, so it is with the inner man. What is the food for the inner man? Not prayer, but the Word of God; not the simple reading of the Word of God, so that it only passes through our minds, just as water runs through a pipe. No, we must consider what we read, ponder over it and apply it to our hearts. What we pray, we speak to God. This exercise of the soul can be best performed after the inner man has been nourished by mediation on the Word of God. Through His Word, our Father speaks to us, encourages us, comforts us, instructs us, humbles us, and reproves us. We may profitably meditate, with God's blessing, although we are spiritually weak. The weaker we are, the more meditation we need to strengthen our inner man. Meditation on God's Word has given me the help and strength to pass peacefully through deep trials. What a difference there is when the soul is refreshed in fellowship with God in the morning. Without spiritual preparation, the service, the trials, and the temptations of the day can be overwhelming." [66]

Muller also advocates reading the Bible with a prayerful, worshipful and meditative spirit. He suggests "the posture of kneeling while praying over the Scriptures." And he *talked* to God

---

[66] Kevin Navarro, 7.

during his Scripture reading; in other words, reading, praying and meditation over the Word, at the same time.

For those Christian ministers who are not setting a solid time and priority for studying the Bible for their own spiritual health, "marinating" in God's Word may be a missing link. Marinating in God's Word—as salt marinates meat —is moving the knowledge, after memorizing and meditating on it, from our head to our heart, a mere 15 inches between head and heart, to become part of our life and influence our behavior.

After passing through my own valley of darkness, I set up a plan to observe, along with my wife, a spiritual retreat every Saturday for two hours, to share what God has taught us that day and that week. Our desire is to discover how much God's Word is actively *marinating* in our lives—adequately mixing through head and heart—seeking areas of life where we did *not* obey God's Word, focusing on thoroughly incorporating this Word into our lives in the days to come. This spiritual discipline is helping us go deeper in our relationship with God, by spending time to understand and connect with our soul by God's Word and God's Grace. My soul is the real me, and holds the motivations that drive all I do. Its core functions are longing, desiring and yearning.

Our conversion is both a point and a process. It is a point when, in that moment, we turn to God. But it is also a process involving the ongoing conversion of our inner person. When we marinate with God's word, he moves in our souls by his grace so that we can produce the fruit of the Holy Spirit.

A unique temptation for Christian ministers studying God's Word is to spend more time reading commentaries and other Christian books than reading the Bible itself. This happened early in George Muller's life; "... he had a love for books yet not for The Book." [67] But over the years, he went deeper in his relationship with

---

[67] Kevin Navarro, 5.

God. Muller weaned himself from his love for books to prefer "the oracles of living God."[68]

A Spiritual X-ray exam helps us understand our spiritual life. Repentance and daily confession in our devotional life keep our spiritual "closets" clean. After a deep cleansing of these unhealthy obstacles, maintaining spiritual health becomes a high priority for Christian ministers.

A prayerful journal of our daily time with God becomes a good record of our spiritual life. It may include our reflections on a portion of the Bible, waiting for the Holy Spirit to pray in us with God's Word, and writing prayer responses to God's Word as we interact with him during this time. This journal may also include daily reminders from God or reflections about the people and circumstances of our day. Daily confession and insight for our souls will also be written. I myself have been blessed by this kind of spiritual practice. I have found the presence of God during various moments of trial and in different seasons of ministry.

When a pastor, missionary or church planner passes through the valley of burnout—from spiritual dryness to a deep cleansing of the root issues of his/her spiritual life—a passion for serving the Lord can be re-ignited as spiritual health is renewed. And he or she can experience spiritual fullness in the days ahead.

---

[68] Ibid., 6.

3

From Insufficient Rest
to Sufficient Rest

Moses, Elijah and Jeremiah all worked hard. They had all been God's servants for a long time, and had all been coping with such high levels of conflict and opposition that they cried out to God, preferring to die rather than continue under those circumstances. This apparent burnout was likely due to insufficient rest, inadequate time management causing an imbalance between work and rest/Sabbath.

Since burnout may be the result of an overloaded ministry, it is natural for us to ask: "Why work?" or "Why minister?" First, both work and ministry are ordained by God. God Himself works as in Genesis 2:2 NIV: "By the seventh day God had finished the work he had been doing." Jesus, as our Redeemer, also worked, first in terms of his mundane years as "a carpenter" (Mark 6:3), then, as He expresses in verses such as John 5:17 NIV "My Father is always at his work to this very day, and I, too, am working." So, God is always working. Work—from the Greek *ergon*—"means God's work over and above his work in creation. It primarily means the acts of Yahweh in history, through which he demonstrates to Israel his covenant-faithfulness. God's deeds include not only preservation and salvation, but also judgment." (e.g. Isa. 28:21.[69])

Moreover, work is required of God's people throughout the Scriptures (Exod. 20:9, 2 Thess. 3:8, 10). The first command to work was given before the fall, because the first couple was to "fill the earth and subdue it." (Gen. 1:28 NIV) So "the Lord God took the man and put him in the Garden of Eden to work it and take care of it." (Gen. 2:15 NIV) The Lord also commanded people to work after the fall, but work became more difficult. Because of the fall the Lord said, "Cursed is the ground because of you; through painful toil you will eat of it." (Gen. 3:17 NIV) This is "the labor and painful toil of our hands caused by the ground the LORD has cursed." (Gen. 5:29 NIV) John Bernbaum and Simon Steer state that, "as a result of the fall, work is no longer the pure joy that God intended it to be. The blessing became a burden and the joy became toil."[70]

From a different perspective, Gordon Lewis and Bruce Demarest state that Christians—including pastors—should "enjoy each day of life on earth, whether they are working or retired. Like the psalmist, they say, 'This is the day the Lord has made; let us rejoice and be glad in it.' " (Ps. 118:24 NIV[71]) They too point out that work is part of God's original plan. Work is "the expenditure of mental and physical energy to the best of our trained abilities in making quality products or doing needed services that we 'have something to share with those in need.' " (Eph. 4:28 NIV[72]) Christ's death on the cross removed the curse, and He re-commissioned His disciples to carry out God's original plan for human beings before the fall.

---

[69] Hans-Christoph Hahn, "Work," in *The New International Dictionary of New Testament Theology*, vol. 3, ed. Colin Brown (Grand Rapids, MI: Zondervan, 1978), 1148.

[70] John A. Bernbaum and Simon M. Steer, *Why Work? Careers and Employment in Biblical Perspective* (Grand Rapids, MI: Baker, 1986), 3.

[71] Gordon R. Lewis and Bruce A. Demarest, *Integrative Theology*, vol. 2 (Grand Rapids, MI: Zondervan, 1990), 63.

[72] Ibid., 65.

The early Christians readily understood surrender to our Lord as slave to master. Everett Ferguson found that "one in five of the residents in Rome was a slave. . . . The slave had no legal rights and was subject to the absolute power of the master."[73] John Madden adds that:

> Though slavery was a prevailing feature of all Mediterranean countries in antiquity, the Romans had more slaves and depended more on them than any other people. ...From such evidence Westermann, Hopkins and others are understandably cautious when attempting to come to a total figure for slaves in the city of Rome in the 1st Century AD. Hopkins' estimate of 300,000–350,000 out of a population of about 900,000–950,000 at the time of Augustus seems plausible.[74]

Moreover, social status was not a concern in Jesus's mind when he said, "Let your light shine before men in such a way that they may see your good works, and glorify your Father who is in heaven" (Matt. 5:16 NASB) So all the credit is due not to the disciples but to the One who creates and redeems them.

Rewards also have their place as a catalyst for hard work, but they may also drive the unfortunate tendency to forgo needed rest in the overly ambitious pursuit of rewards. Reward in the Bible is expressed in terms of wages and payment from both a physical and a spiritual perspective. On the one hand, "God's dealing with sin is sometimes pictured as the paying of wages. The key verse here is Romans 6:23, where wages symbolize the idea that eternal death is

---

[73] Everett Ferguson, *Backgrounds of Early Christianity* (Grand Rapids, MI: Eerdmans, 2003), 59.

[74] John Madden, "Slavery in the Roman Empire: Numbers and Origins," *Classics Ireland* 3 (1996); available at http://www.ucd.ie/classics/96/Madden96.html (accessed Jan 17, 2011)

the appropriate payment for sin, where eternal life is simply a gift."[75] On the other hand, reward can become a positive force driving pastors to become "good and faithful servants." Since crowns are rewards for those who remain faithful to the gospel,[76] Paul awaits the "crown of righteousness" that Christ, the Judge, will award him "on that day." (2 Tim. 4:8 NIV)

Towner explains that, given the symbolism of the crown and physical competition, Paul intertwines again the indicative and imperative of Christian living—what God has done and will do is woven together mysteriously with the possibility and necessity of appropriate human response. In 2 Timothy 4:8, depth is added to the picture of reward by reconfiguring the award setting in eschatological perspective. "...repay him for what he has done." (2 Tim 4:14 NIV) The time frame and setting for this is the eschatological final judgment. To this end, "the Lord" is depicted as "the righteous Judge." Hence the day of reward (and judgment) is identified with the term "that day." (cf. 1:12.[77])

Those who love God and persevere under trial will receive the "crown of life." (James 1:12; Rev. 2:10; 3:11.) Elders who are faithful to the flock will receive "the crown of glory" when the Chief Shepherd appears (1 Pet. 5:4).[78] From the above passages, those crowns will be above and beyond being in heaven.

Actually, the doctrine of reward is evident from Genesis 15:1

---

[75] James C. Wilhoit, Tremper Longman III, and Leland Ryken, ed., *Dictionary of Biblical Imagery*, (Downers Grove, IL: InterVarsity, 1998), s.v. "Wages."

[76] Gordon D. Fee, *The First Epistle to the Corinthians* (Grand Rapids, MI: Eerdmans, 1987), .437. Fee has a different perspective. "The crown "is not some specific aspect of the goal but the eschatological victory itself." Craig L. Blomberg ("Degrees of Reward in the Kingdom of Heaven?" *Journal of the Evangelical Theological Society* 35 [June 1992]: 163) adds that "Eternal life and death are at stake here, not gradations of reward."

[77] Philip H. Towner, *The Letters to Timothy and Titus* (Grand Rapids, MI: Eerdmans, 2006), 616.

[78] James Wilhoit, Tremper Longman III, and Leland Ryken, *Dictionary of Biblical Imagery*, s.v. "Crown."

NIV—where the word of the Lord came to Abram in a vision: "I am your shield, your very great reward"—to Revelation 22:12 NIV where Jesus proclaims: "Behold, I am coming soon! My reward is with me, and I will give to everyone according to what he has done." The Bible distinguishes between earthly and heavenly rewards, physical and spiritual rewards, and the OT and NT concepts of "reward." Old Testament rewards are related to a good life, while the NT vision points to "rewards in the Coming Kingdom . . . as motivation to endure in the faith during trying times. . . . "The prospect of an unseen heavenly reward is offered as a consolation and sustaining hope—an encouragement not to lose heart."[79]

One issue in the OT—the repeated observation that the wicked prosper and the godly suffer—appears to fly in the face of outright divine promises of blessings to the godly. This appears as early as Cain's slaying of righteous Abel. Yet the godly often emerged from their trials strengthened in the fear of God. They were confident that all would be reconciled in Him (Pss. 49:15; 73:15-38; Job 42:1-6). Though they might lose other possessions and blessings, possessing God as their "portion" (reward) made them privileged after all.[80] The Lord Himself, not what He bestows, was the greatest reward, "the portion of my inheritance and my cup." (Ps. 16:5,NKJV[81])

Many recognize distinctions in Jesus' teaching on rewards. First, He integrates reward with a personal relationship with Himself (Mt. 19:29). Second, He teaches degrees in reward, those great and least in the kingdom, and rewards in terms of a greater capacity of service, as over ten cities or five (Luke 19:11-27). Third, reward may be one's fruit, which consists of people, a concept also in Paul's words that the Thessalonians are "my crown of rejoicing." (I Thess. 2:19 KJV) Fourth, reward is superlative, a hundred times as much here and

---

[79] Wilhoit, Longman III, and Ryken, s.v. "Reward."
[80] James E. Rosscup, "Old Testament and New Testament Conceptions of Reward for the Godly" (transcript of paper presented at the Annual Meeting of the Evangelical Theological Society, Toronto, ON, December 28, 1981), 4.
[81] Ibid., 6.

now, and eternal life as well. Fifth, Jesus integrates reward into a context of grace, which Paul develops into the "in Christ" concept, and degrees of reward (I Cor. 3:8; II Cor 9:6). Reward at its very heart is exhilarating fellowship with God in service to His glory. The evangelists and Paul never hint of any disparity between the equality in abundance, yet the differentiation is in degree; that is, reward is in different gradations in reference to each individual's capacity of service, his role, his position, or his rank in particular.[82]

Objections to the doctrine of rewards state that, instead of simply serving the Lord out of love and gratitude, Christians are seeking their own profit, and that this doctrine also promotes pride. If Christians can hope to gain some reward for their faithful obedience, then they would have a reason to boast; they have some gain for which they can take credit. This doctrine is antithetical to a gospel of grace since we are "saved by grace" but "sanctified by works."

Blomberg challenges the entire doctrine and suggests that there are *no* rewards besides eternal salvation. He interprets rewards as that which distinguishes Christians from non-Christians (i.e. salvation), not something that distinguishes Christians from one another.[83] He points out that differences among believers are insignificant, and to expect reward for some above others would be to fail to recognize how we are all similarly unrighteous before God. He adds that rewards would produce a sense of regret and sadness in a place where there is not supposed to be any sadness. Furthermore, if all are perfect in heaven, then it would be illogical to speak about the degrees of perfection. But for Blomberg, the biggest dangers are the implied sense of works-righteousness and the possibility that some might gain false assurance of salvation from their works.

Zane Hodges takes the opposite view that, while salvation is purely a free gift of God, righteous obedience as a Christian results

---

[82] Ibid., 7-9.
[83] Blomberg, "Degrees of Reward," 160.

in reward in Heaven. That is, a fruitless life means the absence of heavenly rewards but not the absence of salvation.[84] Emma Disley adds that the majority of Protestants who expressed convictions on the subject were convinced by the weight of Scriptural evidence that appeared to indicate that there are degrees of reward hereafter. When Calvin rejected the common interpretation of I Cor. 15:41 which applied the verse to the existence of different degrees of honor and glory among the saints, he assured his readers that such a doctrine is nevertheless perfectly true, and is proved by other declarations of Scripture.[85]

Since burnout is related to loss of personal achievement, we would be wise to determine whether the pursuit of reward is biblical or not; is it an end or a means? From the teaching of Jesus, James McDonald concludes that reward is a promise from the Lord, but not a goal.[86] Ramsey elaborates that reward is never action's goal. Reward is always added to the nature of the act, not a direct result of it such as might become a part of the agent's own prudential calculation. If he *were* calculating, the nature of his act would change; it would not be the kind of action for which reward is promised. If he acts for the sake of reward, he has not yet done what God requires of him in readiness for the kingdom, he has not yet become entirely trusting and obedient, not yet single-minded in obedient love.[87]

Therefore, we are both "saved by grace" and we "work by grace" (Eph. 2:10 NKJV). So even if there are degrees of reward, the basic truth about reward is that it is a gift of God's grace to motivate

---

[84] Zane C. Hodges, *Grace in Eclipse: A study on Eternal Rewards* (Dallas, TX: Redencion Viva, 1985), 4-6. Quoted in Paul D. Kim, "Reward and Sanctification" (D.Min. diss.,Westminster Theological Seminary, 2001), 5, note 6.

[85] Emma Disley, "Degrees of Glory: Protestant Doctrine and the Concepts of Rewards Hereafter," *Journal of Theological Studies* 42 (April 1991): 89.

[86] James I. H. McDonald, "The Concept of Reward in the Teaching of Jesus," *Expository Times* 89, no. 9 (1978): 270.

[87] Ibid.

the process of faithful following the Lord, which in itself is not performance-based. This understanding should reduce the risk of motivation by personal achievement as a goal, one of the causes of burnout.

From the perspective of the work of God, the Triune God always works in creation and in redemption. It is God who initiated the plan and designed the timetable for the Israelites to leave Egypt (Exod. 14:13). God also acted to drive out the inhabitants of Canaan before Israel (Exod. 34:10). Throughout the history of Israel, God was always recognized as one who does mighty works and works wonders (Deut. 3:24). The author of John's Gospel underscores the connection between the works of God and the works of Jesus (from the Greek, *ergon* and *ergazomai*). Jesus's motive for everything was a singular purpose: to do the work God had given Him to do (John 4:34), that the works of God might be made manifest (John 9:3). He did God's work but he did it effectively in deed and word (Matt. 11:2; Luke 24:19). Moreover the disciples, as agents of the Gospel for the Lord, were to do even "greater works" than Jesus had done (John 14:12 NKJV).

The difference between faith and work in Paul's epistles is obvious: Righteousness does not come from working to fulfill the law/commandments but by faith alone. On the other hand, while Christ's followers are not saved by good works, they are saved *for* good works (Eph. 2:8-10). Those who work in the ministry are called God's "co-workers" (1 Cor. 3:9 NIV). The service for the Church can be called "work." (Rom. 16:12 NIV) Thus, pastors who are working for the church are doing the "work of the Lord." (1 Cor. 15:58 NIV)

In the NT, *pastor* consists of "shepherd" imagery that "would be meaningful to first-century Christians who would have understood the relationship between sheep and their shepherd. The shepherd was to feed, guide, and protect the sheep, that is to 'oversee' the growth and well-being of the sheep."[88] A pastor must be faithful to Christ the Chief Shepherd (1 Pet. 2:25). Pastoral ministry is a spiritual gift ordained by God. To serve the Lord is an honorable role for the disciples (Luke 22:26), because pastors are called to serve. *Energia* (working, operation, action) is found eight times in Paul's epistles, revealing the divine power that is effective in Christ (Phil. 3:21), in the Holy Spirit (cf. 1 Cor. 12:11), to the apostles (Eph. 3:7), and to the body of Christ (Eph. 4:16).[89] Moreover, Jesus reassured his disciples that he would accompany them to fulfill the Great Commission (Matt. 28:19-20).

As disciples and God's servants, pastors called by God are His fellow-workers (1 Cor. 3:9). Pastors work together with other pastors (Gk. *synergeō*) as colleagues (Gk. *synergos*). In persevering through the circumstances of suffering which "work together for good" (Rom. 8:28, NET), pastors work together with God and other colleagues in the progress of the Kingdom of God (Col. 4:11).

Burnout does not occur simply as the result of a heavy workload but also because of inadequate time for the Sabbath and for rest. The association of Sabbath with creation is found in Gen. 2:1-3 and Exod. 20:11, in the fourth commandment. One monograph seeks "to challenge the view that gives biblical status to this Sunday tradition as binding for the individual or the church, and to challenge the theology that has been developed to give this support."[90] The authors reject both the traditional and the Sabbatarian understandings in the Sabbath/Sunday controversy. Their main argument is that the

---

[88] David A. Mapples, "The New Testament Elder, Overseer, and Pastor," *Bibliiotheca Sacra* 154 (Apr–June 1997): 167.

[89] Hans-Christoph Hahn, "Work," in *The New International Dictionary of New Testament Theology*, vol. 3, ed. Colin Brown (Grand Rapids, MI: Zondervan, 1979), 1152.

[90] A.T.Lincoln, "From Sabbath to Lord's Day: A Biblical and Theological Perspective," in *From Sabbath to Lord's Day*, ed. D. A. Carson (Grand Rapids, MI: Zondervan, 1982), 403.

Mosaic Law is no longer binding on believers, and Christians live for God by fulfilling the law of love and walking in the Spirit.

Under normal circumstances, a day other than Sunday is reserved for pastors to spend time with God, family and others. That day is the pastor's Sabbath. As the true meaning of the Sabbath comes to light, any time of day can serve as Sabbath for pastors, because the same Resurrection that inaugurated our Lord's present reign in power and attested to His deity has also transformed every day into His day.[91] Based on 1 Timothy 1:8-11 and 2 Timothy 3:16-17, the law has a teaching function but must be reinterpreted in light of Christ.[92] For, as Jesus Christ, the Great Shepherd of under-shepherds, points out: "The Sabbath was made for man, not man for Sabbath" (Mark 2:27,NIV). So even though pastors are unable to experience the Sabbath on Sunday because of the nature of their ministry, they can still celebrate their own Sabbath.

There have been different views on "Sabbath" throughout the Church history. Lewis and Demarest argue that, since the Sabbath rest was planned to meet our need for enrichment, workaholics who do not sanctify one day in seven miss its blessings. Those who overwork seven days a week may identify too much with their work and fail to realize the importance of who and what they are as persons. Workaholics devalue the importance of fellowship with their Creator and His people. God himself "blessed the Sabbath day and made it holy" (Exod. 20:11 NIV[93]) Lewis and Demarest appear to follow the "Sunday as Sabbath" view.

Like Aquinas, John Calvin believed that one day in seven should be set aside for worship, based primarily upon God's seventh-day rest at the end of creation. As Calvin points out, "Every seventh day has been especially selected for the purpose of supplying what

---

[91] Ibid., 405.

[92] Mark Timothy Billington, "The Sabbath as a Theological Framework for Leaderhsip Formation" (D.Min. diss., Gordon-Conwell Theological Seminary, 2007), 28-29.

[93] Lewis and Demarest, *Integrative Theology*, 65.

was wanting in daily meditation. First, God rested . . . he dedicated every seventh day to rest, that his own example might be a perpetual rule. . . . [The Lord . . . testifies that he had given, in the Sabbath, a symbol of sanctification to his ancient people (Ezek. 20:12). Spiritual rest is the mortification of the flesh; so that the sons of God should no longer live unto themselves, or indulge their own inclination. So far as the Sabbath was a figure of this rest, I say, it was but for a season; but inasmuch as it was commanded to men from the beginning that they might employ themselves in the worship of God, it is right that it should continue to the end of the world."[94]

Others in the reformation camp developed this position further and argued that the Decalogue commanded such a day of rest and worship:

> The Sabbatarian movement . . . was brought to fruition by the Puritans. The basis for the Sabbatarian understanding is found in the Westminster Confession of Faith. . . . Beckwith and Stott are a contemporary example that argues for the Sabbatarian position. They believe that Sunday, the Christian "Lord's day," is the functional equivalent of Saturday, the Jewish Sabbath, and should be set aside as a day of rest and worship.[95]

Another view is the "Sunday 'as an Appropriate Day' view." Martin Luther stressed that "the observation of a weekly day of rest for worship was not a matter of religious obligation, but he was willing to allow for such a day as a practical necessity for rest and religious instruction. He was even willing to connect this day with Sunday."[96] Luther wrote that:

---

[94] John Calvin, *Commentaries on the First Book of Moses called Genesis*, trans. John King, vol. 1 (Grand Rapids, MI: Eerdmans, 1948), 106-7.
[95] Billington, *Sabbath as a Theological Framework*, 23.
[96] Ibid., 26.

God blessed and sanctified the seventh day. This God did not do with regard to any other creature. From this we are to learn that the seventh day is suitable and should be used especially for public worship. "To sanctify" means to separate (things) from other creatures and to dedicate (them) to God. . . . the meaning of the Sabbath, or the rest of God, is that He (on this day) speaks to us through His Word and we again speak to Him through faith and prayer.[97]

However, his appeal is to tradition and history rather than Scripture: "[S]ince from of old Sunday [the Lord's Day] has been appointed for this purpose, we also should continue the same, in order that everything be done in harmonious order, and no one create disorder by unnecessary innovation."[98]

It is clear from the Old Testament to the New Testament that "the idea of the Sabbath can remind us that we are to be active in worship, whether it is on one particular day, or, more appropriately, every moment of every day."[99] It is God's intention for all his people, including pastors, to share his rest. It is a gift from Jesus Christ, the Great Shepherd, that everyone who believes in Him and who serves Him would share the same "Sabbath rest." For pastors, the principles of Sabbath are no different. If they miss the practice of Sabbath they will lose the needed harmony and balance between work, ministry and rest, and become tired, exhausted, faint and powerless.

"Rest in God" connotes inner peace, the much needed inner peace valued in both the OT and NT. Viewing Matthew 11:28-30 from a pastor's perspective, "weary" evokes an image of emotionally exhausted pastors, burned out in ministry. "Burdened" suggests

---

[97] Martin Luther, *Luther's Commentary on Genesis*, trans. J. Theodore Mueller (Grand Rapids, MI: Zondervan, 1958), 40.

[98] Billington, *Sabbath as a Theological Framework*, 26.

[99] Ibid., 86.

a degree of helplessness under heavy loads. The rest that Jesus the Great Shepherd gives to his disciples, under-shepherds and pastors is dependent upon the relationship they have with Jesus. It is a spiritual rest, a process accompanied by a daily awareness of need. The rest that Jesus gives is realized in pastors' souls—that is, it is a sense of deep existential peace, a shalom, or ultimate well-being as the pastor serves God in obedience to His commandments. The process involves relying on God daily with the humility to be teachable, and accepting God's daily guidance, realizing that only in this way will pastoral ministry be manageable. They can work hard and at the same time regularly experience God's sustaining grace, so they are not crushed or driven to despair (2 Cor. 4:8-9).

Both individuals and congregations frequently view the pastor's calling as a 24/7 commitment. And to explicitly declare or even subtly imply the need for rest as a critical component of effective ministry is interpreted as a less-than-wholehearted commitment to one's calling. In a recent article entitled "Taking a Break from the Lord's Work," Paul Vitello helps us understand the critical importance of scheduling "rest" in the ministry and how the absence of "rest" only promotes burnout and, eventually, drop out:

> These findings have surfaced with ominous regularity over the last few years, and with little notice: Members of the clergy now suffer from obesity, hypertension and depression at rates higher than most Americans. In the last decade, their use of antidepressants has risen, while their life expectancy has fallen. Many would change jobs if they could.
>
> . . . The Clergy Health Initiative, a seven-year study begun by Duke University in 2007, published the first results of a . . . survey of 1,726 Methodist ministers in North Carolina. Compared with neighbors in their census tracts, the ministers

reported significantly higher rates of arthritis, diabetes, high blood pressure and asthma. Obesity was 10 percent more prevalent in the clergy group.

The results echo recent internal surveys by the Evangelical Lutheran Church in America, which found that 69 percent of its ministers reported being overweight, 64 percent having high blood pressure and 13 percent taking antidepressants. A 2005 survey of clergy by the . . . Presbyterian Church also took special note of a quadrupling in the number of people leaving the profession during the first five years of ministry, compared with the 1970s.[100]

Stephen McCutchan, a retired minister in the Presbyterian Church (USA), has witnessed similar tendencies of insufficient rest among clergy: "In my experience, a big resister to care for clergy is the clergy. They feel that it's one more thing that they have to do, and they don't do it well."[101]

By not attending to their physical, mental and spiritual health, clergy are missing an opportunity to care for their congregations:

When they run themselves ragged, they are emulating many members of their congregation. Everyone is time-stressed in this world . . . And how you learn to manage that and also accomplish your purposes is an important balancing act. I think that clergy don't see that as part of their testimony— they see it as extra. They see it as: "after I get my

[100] Paul Vitello, "Taking a Break from the Lord's Work," *New York Times,* Aug 2, 2010.
[101] Stephen McCutchan, quoted in Vitello, "Taking a Break."

work done, I'll have time to do this," as opposed to: "this is part of the importance of my witness."[102]

United Methodist clergy spend 56.2 hours per week in ministry and 12 evenings a month away from home on church duties.[103] While research continues, a growing number of health experts and religious leaders have settled on a simple remedy that has long been a touchy subject with many clerics: "Taking time out."[104] Peter Scazzero got the message and insisted that:

> Each week, we set aside a 24-hour period to keep the Sabbath to the Lord, structuring our time around the following four characteristics of biblical Sabbaths—Stop, Rest, Delight and Contemplate. We also take at least an additional half-day off a week to do the "work" of life and limit our work [at church] . . . .[105]

Insufficient rest clearly contributes to pastoral burnout. Under the pressure of modern fast-paced living, pastors are experiencing a number of challenges in life. In response to societal influence, "The continual pressure of the role of the pastor seems to go on 25 hours a day, 8 days a week."[106] Martha W. Hickman describes our fear of unstructured time: "If I am not working, who am I? If I have free time, will my demons return—those thoughts and fears and possibilities that I am able to sidestep by being busy? Will I feel useless, uneasy? Will something new be expected of me?"[107] Archibald Hart agrees that . . .

---

102 Ibid.
103 Ibid.
104 Ibid.
105 Peter Scazzero, quoted in Vitello, "Taking a Break."
106 Vitello, "Taking a Break."
107 Martha Whitmore Hickman, quoted in Vitello, "Taking a Break."

Ministers tend not to know how to relax. . . . Work that occupies every waking moment for long periods of time—as the ministry often does—can lead to depression. One very common kind of depression in ministers . . . follows the performance of ministerial duties on a Sunday. Sunday afternoons and Monday mornings bring a unique type of depression called the "post adrenaline blues." It is a purely physiological response, but often misunderstood and misinterpreted by the minister. . . . From the beginning of the week the focus is on the Sunday worship or evangelistic service. Sermon preparation, worship service design, hymn selection, visitation of newcomers, and so on—all have Sunday's activities as their goal and culmination. Subtle and often unrecognized anxiety pervades the anticipation of the weekend activity, and there is a gradual but steady buildup of adrenaline in the bloodstream. . . . And then Sunday's activities are over, and there is a massive shutdown of the adrenal system. As a result, the minister is likely to experience a letdown feeling and a period of depression . . . these "post adrenaline" depressions are frequently misunderstood by pastors.

The tendency is to spiritualize the problem and attribute the depression to false causes, and this in turn only compounds the misery of the experience. The best way to deal with these post adrenaline depressions is to allow ample time for rest and recuperation. The depression should not be interpreted as anything but a physiological reaction.[108]

---

[108] Archibald Hart, "Fuller Seminary Study," cited at the Glen Eyrie Conference Center, Colorado Springs, CO, November 7-10, 1991.

Chi Eng Yuan

Journey from insufficient rest to sufficient, holistic rest

Two obstacles to be overcome in order for this journey to advance are the misconception of the *execution* of the Sabbath and a determination of *when* the Sabbath takes place. Rest for Christian ministers in western cultures may be difficult because, despite a deliberate pursuit of leisure, they still experience more fatigue afterward. Conversely, Christian ministers of eastern cultures—more commonly "workaholics" who do not intentionally pursue leisure time—also feel excessive fatigue. Regardless of the physical differences between a five- and seven-day workweek, all have burnout due to insufficient "true" rest.

Regardless of the availability of "time off"—via sabbatical leave, five-day workweeks, pursuit of leisure time, and so on—symptoms of burnout may still remain. A workaholic minister in pursuit of excellence in ministry cannot replace or reduce the power of rest in Christ simply by spending time engaged in entertainment such as watching television, or participating in sports. To self-examine the *significance* of the rest is the first step in this journey.

Christian ministers are able to decide for themselves the time of Sabbath in their ministry. One particular day or period of time is not necessarily better than another, as every day is "the day the Lord has made" (Ps. 118:24 ESV) and "The Sabbath was made for man, not man for the Sabbath" (Mark 2:27 NIV). This flexibility in practicing the biblical truth of Sabbath is particularly relevant in a culture like the Dominican Republic, where pastors typically take no day off after six days of work, but instead set aside periods of rest time *between* their working hours.

After discussing these two obstacles, these questions may be asked: Why do I serve? What really motivates me? Do I feel guilty about taking time off from ministry? If so, why? When is my time of Sabbath?

Judith A. Schwanz, a professor of Pastoral Care and Counseling at Nazarene Theological Seminary, points out that "Sabbath is not a sign of weakness. . . . God not only commanded the Sabbath but also took the very first Sabbath. God didn't need to take a break; but God chose to establish a rhythm of work and Sabbath." [109]

Christian ministers should be suspicious of the excuses they might make in failing to prioritize time for Sabbath. "I just don't have enough time!" "I have other more important things to do!" "I have too many responsibilities to deal with!" "People expect me to be available!" and, "I don't feel like I need a break!"[110]

Christian ministers *do* need rest. In fact, they need five kinds of rest to be renewed, spiritual rest being the most significant one. This, then, is the time to pray: "Embrace us with a tent of Thy peace," rather than, "Guard our going out and our coming in".[111]

Spiritual Rest

Christian ministers can arrange a day for retreat. Setting aside a day to study God's love for Elijah can be quite beneficial. God's recovery plan includes the physical (rest, drink, food), emotional (time to express feelings and companionship), mental (supportive team members), and spiritual (affirmation of God's caring). Elijah's situation (another wounded leader) demonstrates God's medicine for healing four burnout symptoms. During this retreat day, a pastor can read about Elijah's faith journey and learn about healing his or her own lack of faith, in addition to reading and learning from *The Autobiography of George Muller* to learn from this man of faith and love.

Using the time of Sabbath to keep a journal of self-assessment of one's spirituality is highly recommended. In this journal, 13 areas may be considered, as below:

---

[109] Judith A. Schwarz, *Blessed Connection* (Herndon, Virginia:Alban, 2008),162.

[110] Michael Todd Wilson and Brad Hoffmann, *preventing Ministry Failure* (Downers Grave, IL:InterVarsity, 2007), 175-8.

[111] Abraham Joshua Heschel, *The Sabbath* (New York:Farrar, 2005), 23.

1. **Love of God.** In what ways do I love God? Am I closer to God now than I used to be? How? Why or why not?
   a. What is my "picture," "image" or "idea" of what God is really like? How do I "see" or experience God? How has this changed over time?
   b. What is my attitude toward God? Am I humble? Do I argue, or thank, or praise, or question, or curse or confess before God? How real is God to me? How do I handle "dry" or difficult times? How do my human relationships affect my relationship with God?
   c. When do I feel closest to God? Most distant from God? What influences my sense of God's presence? My relationship with him?

2. **Love of Neighbor.** Who are my real neighbors and how do I love them in practice? In what ways do I love the "neighbor" who does not or cannot help or reward me? What is my involvement in justice, mercy or the needs of the poor? Who are my enemies and how do I respond to them? When and what have I sacrificed for people in need? How affirming or how critical of others am I? Do I use or exploit others to meet my own needs? Who am I serving in my life?

3. **Self.** Where or when am I most inclined to think too highly of myself? Too lowly? How do I balance my strengths and my need to rely on God? How grateful am I for who I am, my history, my gifts and abilities? Where am I restless, or joyful, or proud, or burdened, or confident? Am I handling my sexuality in ways pleasing to God? How am I handling power, ambition or pride? How is God at work in me?

4. **Prayer.** When and how do I pray? What progress have I made in learning how to pray? What struggles do I have? What kind of prayer engages me? Where am I willing to seek or find help to grow in prayer?

5. **Practice of Spiritual Disciplines.**
   a. Disciplines of Solitude: Which disciplines do I use often? Seldom? Never? Why or why not? Which ones am I neglecting and why? Which are most nourishing to me? Which help me stretch and grow spiritually?
   b. Disciplines of Community: Which disciplines do I practice with others? Often? Seldom? Never? Why or why not? Which ones am I neglecting? Which ones are most nourishing or helpful to the community and to me?

6. **Works of Flesh/Fruit of Spirit.** Using Galatians 5, list on separate pages the works of the flesh and the fruit of the Spirit. Over several days, ponder one or two items on each list asking: How does this quality or behavior relate to grace? In which areas should I seek help, or rejoice in grace, or find direction or strength? At the conclusion of each reflection time, pray.

7. **What is the balance between grace and guilt in my life?** How is grace growing and guilt losing its power? What place does reliance upon the power of the Holy Spirit have in my life? Where am I now in "faith," "hope" and "love"?

8. **Faithfulness.** What gifts/abilities/passions has God given me and what am I doing with them? Ponder the parable of the talents (Mt. 25) asking: Who am I in this story? What do I expect God to say to me and why? What do I want God to say? Do I need to be doing anything differently than I am doing now?

9. **Integrity.** How good is the match between my public and private life, between what is visible to others and that known only to God? Does my reputation match my reality? How good is my word? Am I trustworthy? Would my life and motives stand scrutiny by others?

10. **Obedience.** How willing am I to do the will of God under ordinary or under difficult circumstances? How diligent am I in seeking to know and do what God commands of me in Scripture and through His Spirit? Am I doing what Jesus tells me to do?

11. **Community.** Am I involved in meaningful, caring Christian community? If married, I loving and faithful? To what extent am I kind, tenderhearted and forgiving in my relationships? Is there anyone of whom I need to ask forgiveness? Anyone I need to forgive? Am I in any relationships of mutual accountability? Is my tongue under control? Do I handle anger well? Am I hospitable?

12. **Money.** What power does money have in my life? What do I do with my money and other resources? Am I a cheerful giver? Are my finances in order with little or no debt? Do I give generously? Do I ever discuss my finances with anyone whom I respect? Am I willing to have other Christians know how I spend money? What place do prayer and biblical principles have in my finances?

13. **Strength and Weakness.** What fears do I have and how do I deal with them? Do I experience the comfort of God in my afflictions? How do I handle weakness and suffering? What do I do with failure? How do I handle success and strength, pressure and stress? Have I faced the reality of my own death? Am I ready to live life fully and face death confidently when it comes by God's grace?

This journal is also a place where we can wrestle with the suffering inherent in ministry. Neither flying from the reality nor fighting against the pain, Christian ministers can walk as Jesus did in his week of crucifixion, as we meditate upon entering the Darkness, walking the way of the Cross and recognizing the Risen Jesus:

- **Entering the Darkness**—"To live at the foot of the cross in daily life means to live in the mess of life without trying to evade it."[112]
- **Walking the Way of the Cross**—"Making this pilgrimage of prayer is to immerse ourselves in the biblical story of Christ's passion, beginning with Jesus's prayer in the garden of Gethsemane."[113]
- **Recognizing the Risen Jesus Christ**—"Record in your journal where you have seen the risen Christ in the context of your own life, especially during times of grief or sorrow, doubt or despair, fear or anxiety, or times when it might have been difficult to recognize Him. Was it a word, a touch, a voice that you heard or a confirmation of what you knew, a sense of peace, an insight, a way forward or a rest? What was this presence like, and how might it speak to whatever is troubling you today?"[114]

In addition, one can choose the spiritual discipline of "Being Still" before God during the period of spiritual rest. The Psalmist advises us to be still and know God (Ps. 46:10). On the other hand, in the course of our normal work, our default reflex is to suppress our true feelings at first. "We can suppress and deny issues for a while, but they can erupt to the surface with explosive and surprising force to dismantle lives. If we regularly take time to be still, it's possible we can deal incrementally with troublesome issues and diffuse their growing destructive power."[115]

For those ministers who have been coping with the dark side of their souls, a time to self-assess reality can be very beneficial—for example, soul-threats in terms of addiction. When you look back

---

[112] Ibid., 118.

[113] Ibid., 120.

[114] Ibid;, 120.

[115] Stephen W. Smith, *Embracing Soul Care* (Grand Rapids, MI:Kregel, 2006), 122.

at your family's history, what patterns of addiction do you see in parents, brothers, sisters, grandparents, aunts and uncles? What surfaces within you as you consider the possibility that you are "hooked" on something? How can you be a *friend* to someone who is hooked on something?

In terms of workaholism, what enticements toward over-work do you see in your national culture? In what ways are workaholics applauded and affirmed? Why? How can you tell if your work life is in balance and not headed toward addictive behavior?[116]

Sabbath is a time to gain emotional rest. The patterns of relating that individual pastors develop in their families of origin shape the way they function in all their relationships. To explore this, a pastor can create a multi-generational genogram beginning with his or her own generation and working backward. The *genogram*, a type of family tree, depicts information regarding the pastor and his or her family. If possible, the pastor should gather information about five generations of the family and include as much of the following information as possible: names, current ages, birth dates, death dates, marriages, divorces, adopted or foster children, pregnancies, miscarriages, stillbirths, abortions, medical conditions (examples include alcoholism and cancer), emotional conditions (examples include anxiety and depression), places of residence, occupations and educational levels.[117]

Assessing one's emotional health can reduce the dangerous consequences of frustration, depression, and apathy which are all related to burnout. Emotions in the pastor's body may be compared to smoke in a chimney: Both have to come out somewhere. Often pastors cannot express or understand fully their own emotions because of their job titles or unrealistic expectations. Peter Scazzero and Warren Bird write that humans are like icebergs in that many

---

[116] Ibid., 190-193.
[117] Richelle Melander and Harold Eppley, *The Spiritual Leader's Guide to Self-Care* (Herndon, VA: Alban Institute, 2002), 78-79.

deep layers are invisible below the surface.[118] Pastors may carry unmet emotional needs that can impact their ministry because they do not take care of their own emotional health. Peter Scazzero, in his book *The Emotionally Healthy Church*, emphasizes, "it is not possible for a Christian [minister] to be spiritually mature while remaining emotionally immature."[119] And "emotional health [the state of emotional rest] is an experience for you when you are alone, and in your close relationships with others."[120]

To help gain understanding about their emotional health, pastors may take a "Levels of Emotional Maturity" test. First, they should evaluate their outward actions to assess what they are feeling and doing. Christ demonstrated emotional intelligence, and pastors can follow his steps. For example, Jesus was deeply moved by and greatly disturbed in his spirit over the death of his friend, Lazarus (John 11). Scazzero and Bird suggest that, if pastors do not know their own inner worlds, they cannot impact the inner worlds of their sheep.[121]

Second, pastors should be serious about breaking generational sin. Pastors can use their genogram to assess the pattern of dysfunction in parts in their family history. Additionally, keeping a journal can help pastors identify their own emotional needs. For example, evaluating how God's grace is sufficient for pastors' weaknesses and blindness may reveal much to the writer. Pastors can learn from Paul how his growth in Christ paralleled his increasing sense of weakness and sinfulness. In Galatians 2:6,NET Paul writes: "But from those who were influential (whatever they were makes no difference to me; God shows no favoritism between people)—those influential leaders added nothing to my message." Later, he asserts: "When I am weak, then I am strong." (2 Cor. 12:10,NASB) Pastors can reflect on a

---

[118] Scazzero and Bird, *The Emotionally Healthy Church*, 72.

[119] Peter Scazzero, *The Emotionally Healthy Church*(Grand Rapids, MI:Zondervan, 2003), 50.

[120] Ibid., 59.

[121] Ibid., 69-78.

regular basis about the development of the emotional truth that to be weak is to be strong in Christ.

Part of discerning emotional maturity involves holding one's self unflinchingly up to impartial assessment. This may begin by soberly looking at a description of emotional maturity levels as assessed by experienced professionals. Scazzero and Bird illustrate the different emotional levels as follows:

- **Emotional infants:** As does a physical infant, I look for other people to take care of me more than I look to care for them. I often have difficulty in describing and experiencing my feelings in healthy ways and rarely enter the emotional world of others. I am consistently driven by a need for instant gratification, often using others as objects to meet my needs, and am unaware of how my behavior is affecting/hurting them. People sometimes perceive me as inconsiderate, insensitive and self-centered.

- **Emotional children:** As with a physical child, when life is going my way and I am receiving all the things I want and need, I am content and seem emotionally well adjusted. However, as soon as disappointment, stress, tragedy or anger enter the picture, I quickly unravel inside. I interpret disagreements as personal offenses and am easily hurt by others. When I don't get my way, I often complain, throw an emotional tantrum, withdraw, manipulate, drag my feet, become sarcastic or take revenge. I have difficulty calmly discussing with others what I want and expect from them, in a mature, loving way.

- **Emotional adolescents:** As do physical adolescents, I know the right ways I should behave in order to "fit into" mature, adult society. I can feel threatened and alarmed inside when I am offered constructive criticism, quickly becoming defensive. I subconsciously keep records on the love I give out, so I can ask for something in return at a later time. When I am in conflict, I might admit some fault in the matter, but I will insist on demonstrating the guilt of the other party, proving why they are more to blame. Because of my commitment to self-survival, I have trouble really listening to another person's pain, disappointments or needs without becoming preoccupied with myself.

- **Emotional adults:** I can respect and love others without having to change them or becoming critical and judgmental. I don't expect anyone to be perfect in meeting my relational needs, whether it is my spouse, parents, friends, boss or pastor. I love and appreciate people for who they are as whole individuals, the good and the bad, and not for what they can give me or how they behave. I take responsibility for my own thoughts, feelings, goals and actions. When under stress, I don't fall into a victim mentality or a blame game. I can state my own beliefs and values to those who disagree with me—without becoming adversarial. I am able to accurately self-assess my limits, strengths, and weaknesses and freely discuss them with others. Deeply in tune with my own emotions and feelings, I can move into the emotional worlds of others, meeting them at the place of their feelings, needs and concerns. I am deeply convinced that I am absolutely loved by Christ, that I have nothing to prove.[122]

In this emotional-rest retreat, Christian ministers can follow the six principles Scazzero recommends which include looking beneath the surface, breaking the power of the past, living in brokenness and vulnerability, receiving the gift of limits, to embrace grieving and loss, and making incarnation one's model for loving well.[123]

Ray S. Anderson points out clearly that "feelings may be the most critical indicators of well-being that we possess. The feelings

---

[122] Ibid., 66.
[123] Ibid., 6.

that we acquire as infants and children form the matrix of the self for our adult years. Feelings need care and nurturing as much, if not more, than the physical part of the self. When our feelings are sick, there is no health in us. And without feelings, we have no contact with the world and no relationship with others. Feelings are an essential and accurate expression of the self. Far from being a deterministic factor of the human personality, emotions are capable of transformation and change. Emotion represents the creative possibility of growth and change in the recovery of self." [124] In other words, listen intentionally to what our emotions tell us and write down what we hear.

Choosing one kind of emotion, praying and searching for deep healing will be a fruitful experience for Christian ministers during their special day or period of rest in Him.

Pastor Scazzero recommends a "structure of rest" in the life of his pastoral team at New Life Fellowship, a holistic rest approach, as below:

Rest

- **Sabbath**—Each week, we set aside a 24-hour period to keep the Sabbath to the Lord, structuring our time around the following four characteristics of biblical Sabbaths: *stop, rest, delight* and *contemplate*. We also take at least an additional half-day off a week to do the "work" of life and limit our work at New Life Fellowship. We trust God to build his church and respect Sabbath-keeping as an essential formation discipline in our lives.
- **Simplicity**—We model percentage giving (using the tithe as a minimal guideline) in giving to God's work here at New Life Fellowship. We manage our material resources in a manner that honors God and avoids the traps and

---

[124] Ray S. Anderson, *Self Care* (Wheaton, ILL:Victor, 1995), 64-9.

enticements of Western culture (e.g. bad debt, gambling, etc.) as we live out the basic principles of our Good Sense Course (i.e. giving, saving, budgeting, balancing a spending plan, and planning).

- **Play and Recreation**—We have a life outside of New Life Fellowship for balance and health. We recognize the seasons and rhythms of leadership and the church year and plan compensatory breaks accordingly. We build healthy "fun" into our discipleship and take vacations each year to allow the soil of our lives to be replenished and receive fresh "nutrients" from God as we take mini-sabbaticals along the four principles of stopping, resting, delighting and contemplating.[125]

After spiritual and emotional rest, physical rest becomes a critical burnout factor. Christian ministers can take some important steps to prevent their bodies from getting worn out. First, they can eat sensibly. God created the human body to require food in reasonable amounts and appropriate balance ideal for proper digestion, distribution of nutrients, and elimination of wastes. Table 1 is a tool for achieving this balance, listing the "good" carbohydrates, proteins, and fats.[126]

---

[125] Pete Scazzero, *Pastoral Staff Rule of Life* (Elmhurst, NY: New Life Fellowship, 2008), 2.

[126] Ben Lerner, *Extreme Makeover God's Way* (Kissimmee, FL: Body by God, 2004), 24-26.

Chi Eng Yuan

Table 1. A Tool for Achieving Nutritional Balance

Good Carbohydrates, Good Proteins, and Good Fats	
Good Carbohydrates: Fruits	apples, bananas, blackberries, blueberries, cantaloupe, currants, grapes, grapefruit, honeydew, kiwi, lemons, limes, mango, oranges, peaches, pears, pineapple, plums, prunes, nectarines, raisins, raspberries, tangerines, watermelon
Good Carbohydrates: Whole Grains	cream of brown rice, other hot whole grain cereals (barley, quinoa, rye, spelt, millet), rice (brown, basmati, and jasmine), rice cakes, rice noodles, puffed rice cereal, breads and flours (all-natural, whole grain, sugar-free), gluten-free and sprouted breads, barley, buckwheat, rye, spelt, millet, quinoa, oats, grits
Good Carbohydrates: Starchy Vegetables	corn, peas, potato, squash, sweet potato
Good Carbohydrates: Vegetables	alfalfa, artichoke, arugula, asparagus, bamboo shoots, beets, broccoli, brussels sprouts, cabbage, carrots, cauliflower, celery, collard greens, cucumber, eggplant, escarole, green beans, kale, lettuce, mesclun, mustard greens, onions, parsley, parsnips, pea pods, radish, radicchio, scallion, seaweed, shallots, swiss chard, snap peas, snow peas, spinach, string beans, tomato, turnips, watercress, wheat grass, zucchini
Good Proteins: Beans	chickpeas, kidney, lentil, lima, navy, pinto and white beans
Good Proteins: Nuts	almonds, hazelnuts, macadamia, pine nuts, walnuts

Good Carbohydrates, Good Proteins, and Good Fats	
Good Proteins: Eggs	organic, free-range
Good Proteins: Fish	grouper, halibut, mackerel, mahi-mahi, salmon, sardines, sea bass, snapper, swordfish, tuna, trout, whitefish
Good Proteins: Poultry	organic, free-range chicken and turkey breast
Good Proteins: Red Meat	organic, grass-fed beef, lean beef
Good Fats	olives, olive oil (cold-pressed, extra-virgin), extra-virgin coconut oil, organic fats (grass and vegetable-fed beef, egg yolks, and chicken), crushed seeds, tahini, fish oil, almonds, walnuts, avocado, macadamia nuts

Table 2: A worksheet for tracking nutritional balance.[127]

Daily Diet Diary   Date: _____

Time	Substance & Amount	Right Food	Carbohydrate, Protein, or Fat	Why You Are Eating	How You Feel 1 Hr. Later

God asks His follows to honor Him with their bodies (1 Cor. 6:20). In the first week of this program, Christian ministers identify the foods they eat using the diet diary above for seven consecutive days. Additionally, we plan a sensible exercise routine such as a brisk walk, jogging, swimming, bicycling, roller blading, or using some kind of cardio equipment. We then pray for the means to maintain a balanced food plan and perform our simple exercise activity for at least 30 minutes at least four times per week. Regular aerobic movement can be effective in as little as ten to fifteen minutes, and resistance movement can be effective in as little as three minutes.[128] Exercising in appropriate ways five days per week can improve a pastor's health and fitness levels. Pastors, church planers, missionaries and Christian leaders can keep a record of heart rate and fat burning, and evaluate improvement on a semi-annual or annual basis.

On the following pages, Figure 5 provides information on target heart rates, Figure 6 suggests action steps for the program,[129] and Figure 7 is a worksheet with which pastors may track their progress.[130]

---

[128] Ibid.
[129] Ibid., 71.
[130] Ibid., 80.

Chi Eng Yuan

Calculating Your Moving Zone Heart Rates

Maximum Heart Rate (MHR) = 220 – Your Age

Fat Utilization Rate (FUR) = 55-75% MHR

Performance Enhancement Rate (PER) – 75-85% MHR

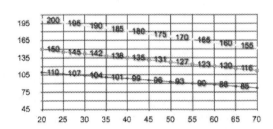

For Fat Burning Rates (FUR and PER):

- Increase by five beats if you are regularly exercising.
- Increase by 10 beats if you are an experienced athlete.
- Lower by five beats if you are just starting out.
- Lower by 10 beats if you are on medication or recovering from injury or illness.

Sugar Utilization Rate (SUR) = 85-95% of MHR

Example Calculation for Determining Moving Zone Heart Rates

Age: 40

    MHR: 220 – 40 = 180 BPM

    Fat Burning Rates:

    FUR = 55-75% OF 180 = 99 – 135 BPM

    PER = 75-85% OF 180 = 135 – 153 BPM

    SUR = 85-95% OF 180 = 153 – 171 BPM

Figure 5. Target Heart Rate Information

Action Steps for Today

Using your moving zones, find the speed and energy output necessary to get to the FUR level during exercise.

Do a 5 – 5 – 5 (or at least a 5 – 5) workout at least two days a week.

- 5 – 5 – 5 = 5-minute warm up, 5 minutes at FUR, 5-minute cool down.
- 5 – 5 = 5-minute warm up and 5 minutes at FUR.
- "Overnight Success" Plan: a 5 – 15 – 5 workout.

Find your ideal moving zones on the chart above and write them below.

My FUR: _____

My PER: _____

My SUR: _____

Figure 6. Action Steps to Improve Heart Health

Fat Burning   Personal Aerobic Routine

Example 30 Minute Cardiovascular Movement (+10 Minute Warm-up/Cool Down = 40 Minute Total)

Name:_____ Age:_____ Gender: M / F

Activity:_____

> WARNING – BEFORE YOU BEGIN: Never start an exercise program without first consulting your physician. Those with a personal history of heart disease, high blood pressure, high cholesterol, cancer, diabetes, or who smoke or are overweight should begin exercise with professional supervision.

FUR = FAT UTILIZATION RATE
PER = PERFORMANCE ENHANCEMENT RATE
SUR = SUGAR UTILIZATION RATE

MOVING ZONE LEVELS FUR: _____ PER: _____
SUR: _____

TIME ELAPSED TIME	TIME PER STAGE	HEART RATE	SPEED/INCLINE OR LEVEL/RPM	HEART RATE REAL
0:00	0:00	Resting Heart Rate (RHR)+	MPH/	
5:00	5:00	Below – FUR	MPH/	
7:00	2:00	Near – FUR	MPH/	
9:00	2:00	Nearer – FUR	MPH/	
11:00	2:00	First 1% - FUR	MPH/	
13:00	2:00	First 50% - FUR	MPH/	
15:00	2:00	First 50% - PER	MPH/	
17:00	2:00	SER	MPH/	
19:00	2:00	PER – FUR	MPH/	
21:00	2:00	PER	MPH/	
24:00	3:00	PER – FUR	MPH/	
26:00	2:00	Last 50% - PER	MPH/	
28:00	2:00	PER	MPH/	
32:00	4:00	SUR	MPH/	
34:00	2:00	PER – FUR	MPH/	
36:00	2:00	PER	MPH/	
41:00	5:00	SUR	MPH/	
45:00	4:00	PER – FUR	MPH/	
50:00	5:00	FUR = RJR +		

Figure 7. Worksheet to Track Heart Health Progress

It is difficult for many Christian servants of God to get adequate sleep. Brooks Faulkner, author of *Burnout in Ministry*, reveals that sleep is the body's renewal program. Christian leaders can assess their body's need for sleep by recording all time spent sleeping during a vacation period (when daily activities aren't exerting artificial constraints), then dividing the total of sleep hours by the days of the vacation, to determine hours of sleep needed per day—taking care, then, to not *over*sleep going forward.[131] Minimizing the importance of this aspect of physical maintenance can actually harm a caregiver's overall health.

---

[131] Faulkner, *Burnout in Ministry*.

From Incompatibility to Compatibility with Ministry

When a pastor is at odds over his job description with those who hired him, an inevitable sense of incompatibility occurs. This only aggravates emotional exhaustion, a symptom of burnout. It is time for those pastors, church planners or missionaries to review God's calling. He is the one who provides strength for his servants to meet the needs of the sheep. He never leaves a pastor without the resources he or she needs to fulfill their calling. The pastor must wrestle with Jesus's call for His disciples to be "servants of the Lord". Spiritual authority and leadership come only through the path of suffering and sacrifice (Mark 10:38-39). For example, while Paul may have had all the status of a VIP, he did not abuse his leadership position but served humbly. (2 Cor. 3:9; 11:26-29).

Incompatibility with ministry may occur when an individual does not appreciate the true nature of the pastorate or the extent of his personal gifts and/or limitations. Most pastors believe themselves to be inferior and incapable of facing the challenges because 1) they have doubts about their callings; 2) the particular pastoral position comes with an overwhelming job description; and 3) lay leaders and congregations reinforce the natural tendency to put pastors on pedestals.

Incompatibility with Ministry

Don Cousins, former staff member of Willow Creek mega-church in Chicago, argues that North American churches have been caught up in worldly models of success which include honoring superstar CEOs and pursuing the elusive gift of leadership, as defined by certain Christian-leadership gurus.[132] This kind of focus could well lead to even more burnout due to incompatibility, because congregations and lay leaders tend to compare their pastors with these "big names," making it impossible for them to fulfill expectations. The difference between experiencing this unfortunate *"Catch-22"* and effective pastoral ministry depends on whether pastors clearly know their calling, for incompatibility in the pastorate seems intertwined with a confusion of the pastoral call.

Church history reveals four historical periods of "calling": the call to Christian Life in the Early Church, religious vocations in the Middle Ages, seeing every job as a vocation in the Reformation, and vocation in a Post-Christian Age.[133] Accurately identifying the pastoral call thus depends strongly on the nature of God's call, which may not be to the pastorate. A diligent search for one's true calling is thus critical to understand why a pastor might be suffering from symptoms of burnout, or to help prevent pastoral burnout altogether. And it is equally significant in the decision of whether to stay in or leave a church.

The "calling" (Gk. *kaleō*) is a divine invitation to vocation, and it brings pastors into His service. Romans 4:17 says that God calls us to a brand new existence, nothing short of a new creation; it is "a process by which God calls those, whom God has already elected and appointed, out of their bondage to this world, so that

---

[132] Don Cousins, *Experiencing Leader Shift: Letting Go of Leadership Heresies* (Colorado Springs, CO: David C. Cook, 2008), 20-21.

[133] William C. Placher, ed., *Callings* (Grand Rapids, MI: Eerdmans, 2005), 5-10.

he may justify and sanctify them." (Rom. 8:29-30)[134] The expected transformation from sinner to saint is the work of God through Jesus's blood. According to Peter's First Epistle, we are called out of darkness (1 Pet. 2:9) by following the example of Christ even in suffering (2:21).[135] It is therefore essential for prospective pastors to realize the radical change involved before accepting the call to be a pastor.

John C. Hutchison, an associate professor of Bible exposition at Talbot School of Theology, points out that Jesus called the disciples to be servants of the Lord and reminds us that spiritual authority and leadership come only through the path of suffering and sacrifice (Mark 10:38-39).[136] Jesus thus presented a new model for pastoral identity—a servant leadership that was "one of the most difficult commands for [the disciples] to understand and obey in their cultural situation. This radical call demanded deep personal humility and violated foundational cultural values related to honor/shame and patronage that were embedded in Jewish and Greco-Roman society."[137]

The Apostle Paul exemplified this healthy sense of servanthood. In his book *Apostle of the Crucified*, Michael J. Gorman finds that Paul is not merely a "traveling preacher" and "community builder," but is also called to be a suffering servant: "For Paul, suffering was one way of identifying with his Lord, or reliving his story in the present. His suffering was also, therefore, like Jesus's death, an act of love for those to whom he preached. . . . Ultimately this was the

---

[134] Lothar Coenen, "Calling," in *The New International Dictionary of New Testament Theology*, ed. Colin Brown, vol. 1 (Grand Rapids: Zondervan, 1979), 275.

[135] Ibid., 276.

[136] John C. Hutchison, "Servanthood: Jesus' Countercultural Call to Christian Leaders," *Bibliotheca Sacra* 166 (Jan-Mar 2009): 54.

[137] Ibid.

cost of apostleship."[138] Yet Paul's letters indicate that he did not have a naturally passive personality conducive to servanthood; he had to work to develop humility and a servant's heart (2 Cor. 11:16-29).

Paul's servitude included physical suffering: "in hard work and toil, through many sleepless nights, in hunger and thirst, many times without food, in cold and without enough clothing" (2 Cor. 11:27 NET), as well as exhaustion due to emotional needs, as detailed in 2 Cor. 11:28-30. The daily assault of incoming reports regarding the churches he had established fed his sense of anxiety; these churches, however, also brought him joy. In addition being drained by physical and emotional exhaustion, Paul also coped with spiritual hardships. He wrote, "Who is weak, and I am not weak? Who is made to fall, and I do not burn?" (2 Cor. 11:29,NIV). Yet Paul did not suffer from burnout syndrome, because he maintained the perspective that his suffering was to emulate Christ's. Paul articulated a philosophy of weakness based on Christ's humility (Phil. 2:5-9), even boasting of his incompetence because of a positive view of what weakness accomplished in his life.

Paul thus viewed his pastoral ministry and suffering as an authentic extension of Jesus's own suffering (Col. 1:26). His catalogue of sufferings resulted from his missionary travels and the daily pressure of anxiety, factors that can cause burnout. The sufferings detailed in 2 Corinthians 11:23b-33—labors, imprisonments, floggings and exposure to death—show that Paul's suffering for Christ may well have been more hazardous than the symptoms suffered by contemporary pastors of unrealistic expectations, incompatibility, lack of confidants and spiritual dryness.

Paul's ministry was effective but for a period of time he had to serve as a bi-vocational minister. "Labors" were necessary because Paul steadfastly refused payment from the likes of the church of Corinth, choosing to offer the gospel freely. Paul Barnett, a teaching

---

[138] Michael J. Gorman, *Apostle of the Crucified Lord* (Grand Rapids, MI: Eerdmans, 2004), 70.

Chi Eng Yuan

fellow at Regent College, Vancouver, points to 2 Corinthians 11:8-10 where Paul, in order not to be an obstacle in sharing the Good News . . .

> . . . was determined that the Corinthians should contribute nothing toward the ministry they received. On the one hand he "lowered" himself (by self-support) to preach the gospel "free of charge" to them. Paul summarizes his determination that "in all things" he will be financially independent of the Corinthians. Paul's sufferings are inextricably connected with his "labor" in support of himself. Such labor in self-support, by which he "lowered" himself, was a sign legitimating his unique apostolicity. God had called him to this specific "field" of ministry (10:15-16) and since it was a matter of obedience, he could not be paid.[139]

This was the badge of his apostolate to the Gentiles that the false teachers could not wear, because they accepted payment. No doubt if Paul had accepted the patronage of these churches—protection, payment, and gifts—many of the sufferings on his list would not have occurred. Thus, refusal to accept such patronage and his attendant need to "labor" not only marked his divine apostolate but also contributed significantly to his sufferings.

By the same token, Ben Witherington, Professor of New Testament for Doctoral Studies at Asbury Theological Seminary, concedes the balance of "giving and receiving" in Philippians 4:10-20. Paul is willing to "receive [the Philippians church's gift] in full," because "it is God who began a relationship with the Philippians. . . .

---

[139] Paul Barnett, *The Second Epistle to the Corinthians* (Grand Rapids, MI: Eerdmans, 1997), 515-19.

In Paul's mind generous giving is an act of worship to God."[140] His relationship with the Philippians was a long-term friendship and cooperation for Paul in fulfilling the commission to spread the gospel. That is why their gifts are a "fragrant and pleasing offering to God."[141] Paul was deeply touched by the love and kindness of the church at Philippi, so the gift sent by the hand of Epaphroditus "is the highest value in the sight of God: it was 'an acceptable sacrifice, pleasing to God.' (Phil. 4:18, NIV). No higher praise could be given."[142]

While Paul demonstrated the humble mindset of a lowly slave of Christ, he did not minimize the key role his ministry had in the growth and development of the church at Corinth; after all, it was Paul himself "through whom you came to believe" (1 Cor. 3:5a, NIV). Paul did not lord his apostleship over the churches for his own ambition but he did "claim authority and status as an Apostle over the congregations he founded. . . . He is the founder, the father, the one whose activity brought them into the Christ-movement."[143] Paul depicts the particulars of his role as given to him "not as a means in themselves but as tools to serve the Christ-movement, Christ, and, in and through these, to serve God (II Cor. 3:9)."[144]

Therefore, when Paul urged the Corinthians to imitate him (1 Cor. 4:16), he acted selflessly out of a desire to expand the Church. Paul wanted to give the Corinthians an example or model of how they should act as followers of Christ. His instruction was not driven by a selfish desire for power. In Paul's thinking, it is "the

---

[140] Ben Witherington, *Friendship and Finances in Philippi* (Valley Forge, PA: Trinity Press International, 1994), 131-32.

[141] Gordon Fee, *Paul's Letter to the Philippians* (Grand Rapids, MI: Eerdmans, 1995), 425-26 (emphasis added).

[142] Peter T. O'Brien, *The Epistle to the Philippians* (Grand Rapids, MI: Eerdmans, 1991), 515.

[143] Kathy Ehrensperger, *Paul and the Dynamics of Power* (New York: T & T Clark, 2007), 144.

[144] Ibid., 147.

responsibility he feels (grounded in the durative nature of the gospel) to the authority he manifests (grounded in the weakness and power of the word of the cross), and manifest in the apostle"[145] with the Pauline understanding of apostolic authority that "power is the source of authority, and authority is a version of power as it interprets power and makes it accessible."[146] Paul had a calling to fulfill God's claim on a human life—one that displayed a healthy self-image and maintained the delicate balance between apostolic authority and servant leadership.[147]

This balance can be a daunting challenge for confident and determined contemporary pastors; it is essentially gaining the maturity of wisdom. As a pastor, Paul prayed and asked God to fill his flock with knowledge of His will through all spiritual wisdom and understanding (Col. 1:9). Paul's example demonstrated that the spiritual wisdom of focus on Christ involves knowing God and being aware of one's own value in Christ, as well as the willingness to be called as a suffering servant pastor. Consequently, contemporary pastors can emulate Paul's example and apply God's words whenever they encounter unfair, unpredictable, unsolvable and frustrating moments in ministry.

Could a misconception of the role of the pastor contribute to incompatibility? In Ephesians 4:11, "pastor" appears only in the context of local church leadership. What are the roles of a pastor with regard to the rest of the body of Christ? The verb "to pastor" occurs four times in describing the activity of elders who are to feed the church (John 21:16, Acts 20:28, 1 Cor. 9:7, and 1 Pet. 5:2), but the noun "pastor" is used interchangeably with "elder" and "overseer"

---

[145] John Howard Schütz, *Paul and the Anatomy of Apostoic Authority* (Louisville, KY: Westminster John Knox, 2007), 242.

[146] Ibid., 21.

[147] Andrew D. Clarke, *A Pauline Theology of Church Leadership* (New York: T & T Clark, 2008), 102-103.

to emphasize various functions of the same office.[148] The overseers identified as elders in Acts 20:28 were also enjoined to shepherd ("pastor") the flock.[149] The term "elders" stresses godly wisdom and maturity, "overseers" points to oversight and rule, while "pastors" connotes feeding and tending the flock.[150]

Incompatibility with the ministry may occur when an individual understands neither the true nature of the pastorate nor his personal limitations and/or gifts. Some pastors have an attractive appearance, impressive rhetorical skills, great memory for names and personal histories, and the charisma necessary to draw attention and be easily accepted by the congregation.[151] But most believe themselves to be inferior and incapable of facing the challenges and fulfilling the pastoral role well.

Gary L. McIntosh, professor of Christian Ministry and Leadership at Talbot School of Theology, Biola University, and Robert L. Edmondson, author of *It Only Hurts on Monday*, found that 27 percent of pastors have doubts about their callings, as in the following example:

> Joe was in his early forties and had been a practicing dentist for fifteen years. When he became dissatisfied with his role as a layman, Joe's pastor interpreted his dissatisfaction as an indication that God was calling him into "full-time Christian service." Without serious consideration of Joe's gifts, his pastor advised him to go to seminary. . . . It soon became obvious that he could not handle the academic pressures. Moreover, in his homiletics class he

---

[148] David A. Mapples, "The New Testament Elder, Overseer, and Pastor," *Bibliotheca Sacra*, 154 (Apr-June 1997): 164.

[149] Ibid., 167.

[150] Ibid., 169.

[151] Melody H. Newton and Richard A. Hurt, *The Psychology of Clergy* (Harrisburg, PA: Morehouse, 1991) 126.

found that he could not organize his thoughts into a sermon, nor could he get up before an audience without becoming panic-stricken. Before long, Joe was in a serious state of depression. Thankfully, the supportive dean of students recognized Joe's trouble and helped him realize that what he had interpreted as God's call to a church related vocation was based largely on the false assumption that to be a first-class Christian he needed to be a pastor.[152]

The job description of a 21st Century pastor produces overwhelming and self-defeating expectations for performance:

To comfort the sick and dying, to be the tower of strength for the bereaved and/or the anxious bridegroom, to counsel the maritally afflicted, to pray at a moment's notice, to be all-wise in the problems of child care and in-family jousting, to administer a [large] budget, to raise money for loan payments without issuing bonds, to run a church program efficiently with an all-volunteer staff that serves when it feels like it, to act as building and grounds maintenance supervisor, to prepare miraculously and preach eloquently, to dress meticulously but not too well, to be a saint in all interpersonal relationships with language that even your grandmother would not question, to love his children and see that they are raised in an exemplary manner, to keep his own marriage and personal habits above question, to be never grossly . . . in

---

[152] Gary L. Mcintosh and Robert L. Edmondson, *It Only Hurts on Monday* (Carol Stream, IL: Church Smart Resources, 1998), 29.

debt, and to set a pattern of living that all can follow in faith and spiritual development.[153]

Pastors may feel incompetent when faced with such a broad range of demands and challenges, even if they consider themselves effective leaders.

In 2006 the Barna Group reported that "more than nine out of ten senior pastors of Protestant churches said they now consider themselves to be effective leaders, but only one out of every seven senior pastors say they are effective at thinking and acting strategically."[154] Pastors may feel the stress of mental exhaustion because lay leaders and congregations tend to put pastors on pedestals, and as a result they have a difficult time fulfilling their responsibilities. One in five pastors responding to the Barna Group's survey stated they were not meeting congregational demands, and 25 percent believed they were mismatched with their congregation. Although they may have fit in with their church at an earlier stage, the culture and needs of the congregation changed.[155] Similar dynamics contributed to the resignations of 43 percent of pastors in the McIntosh and Edmondson survey.[156]

Compatibility in Ministry

Could a biblical view of ministry provide the foundation for Christian ministers to establish compatibility in *their* ministries? Two Graces from above are God's gift of salvation and God's gift of ministry. Christian ministers are to be managers of grace. Grace

---

[153] Ruth Truman, *Underground Manual for Ministers' Wives (and Other Bewildered Women)* (Nashville, TN: Abingdon, 1974), 26.

[154] George Barna, "Church Leaders Emphasize Motivation, but Struggle with Strategy" (The Barna Group, February 2006), available at www.barna.org. (accessed April 17, 2007).

[155] Ibid.

[156] McIntosh and Edmondson, *It Only Hurts on Monday*, 19.

connects, enlists and empowers. God's power at work in us (cf. I Cor. 15:10) can be considered The Theology of Grace. We become stewards of grace, responsible for showing others how it works. Grace engages us, calls us, pushes, develops us and gives us a ministry.

Ministry originates in and is the expression of God's grace. Ministry is the free flow of grace from God through us to other people. The Pastor has the special role of being the steward of God's grace given through explaining, demonstrating and dispensing it. Christian ministers respond to the grace of God by following daily the crucified Messiah and taking up their own crosses. They deny their own interests by "Seeking first his kingdom and his righteousness"(Matt 6:33 NIV), and making disciples of all nations (Matt 28:19-20). Along with these two priorities, Christian ministers will develop "godly worry", as Paul worried about the churches (2 Cor. 11:29). Paul used all his mind and heart for our Lord's churches and God caused the church to grow and bear fruit. In other words, Christian ministers cannot master their ministry by themselves because "only God can make the plant grow and bring forth fruit." (I Cor. 3:7, NIV.) Serving God, relying on Him wholeheartedly and increasing our passion to be gracious to others by God's grace are interwoven without comprising our competence. In order to cope with the challenge of compatibility in ministry, Christian ministers are encouraged to review a biblical view of ministry once a week, remembering that ministry is a grace from above. We pursue the best, while understanding that the minister is but a tool. It is God who works in and through us.

Can a deep and honest review of one's calling to be a Christian minister rescue and re-ignite someone to serve Him wholly again? Understanding the Calling of God to Motivate Ministry is one of the key ingredients to again serve the Lord passionately.

For many Christian ministers, it is easy to lose the joy of ministry. It becomes drudgery, unless they understand and allow the calling of God to motivate their ministries. Ministers must pay attention to

God's will and His calling.[157] If the minister is motivated to please others more than God, he may lose his ministry. On the other hand, if the minister does not consider the demands of others, but only considers his own personal goals and desires, he may fall into the sin of pleasing only himself. His motivation for ministry must come from understanding the calling of God.

For example, in John 11:1-7, Martha was very upset with Jesus because He did not get to Bethany when her brother was still sick. If He had arrived there earlier, Lazarus would not have died. Jesus waited two days after hearing about Lazarus's illness before traveling to Bethany. While Jesus loved Mary and Martha dearly, it was evident that He did not set His agenda based on the desires of those to whom He ministered, but according to God's will and His calling.

Likewise, in John 2, at the wedding feast at Cana where Jesus performed His first miracle—that of turning water into wine—He responded to His mother's request by saying, "Woman, ...my time has not yet come." (John 2:4, NIV) Jesus made it clear to Mary His mother that He would perform this miracle not according to her demands, but those of God, the Father. The point is that the focus of ministry is not on the demands of the congregation, but rather on God's calling and His demands. So re-visiting God's calling in the ministry can sustain Christian ministers' persistence and stamina to serve the Lord.

These days, electronic media such as email, e-books, e-connects, Facebook and the like seem to have become more important than the Bible. We depend on new ideas, new strategies, new handbooks and new paradigms. When we replace bearing our own cross with "having fun" in seemingly any circumstance, "Taking up the Cross" becomes less or unimportant for ministers of the Gospel of Grace. Cruciformity, the daily life of making the Cross the center of our life and our ministry, will increase our compatibility in ministry when

---

[157] Sung Hee Lee, "Pastor's Self Management", *Ministry and Theology* (November 1998), 125.

we truly realize and surrender to God's will that Christian ministers are called to suffer and to serve Him with humility.

"The sin of pride is the oldest one in the Book."[158] Whether mild or serious, it starts with vanity, a preoccupation with one's appearance or image that can be tested: When we look at a group photo, do we look first at ourselves? Do we look only at ourselves? Then come's stubbornness, which causes us to ". . . shun correction. It renders us unable to stop defending ourselves. When someone points out an error or flaw, we evade or deny or blame someone else."[159] The deepest, most critical problem with pride lies in its "comparative nature," that of "looking down on everybody else,"[160] breaking God's commandments to love God and to love others as ourselves. This is a serious me-only sin.

On the other hand, "Humility has to do with submitted willingness. It involves a healthy self-forgetfulness . . . by the Holy Spirit to live in the moment that we cease to be preoccupied with ourselves one way or the other. When we are with others, we are truly with them, not wondering how they can be of benefit to us. . . . Humility is the freedom to stop trying to be what we're not, or pretending to be what we're not, and accepting our 'appropriate smallness.' It is to stop being the prodigal son without turning into the elder brother."[161]

When Jesus came in the form of a servant, he was not disguising who God is, but *revealing* who God is, by helping those in urgent need who did not necessarily contribute to his ministry. Moreover, the ministry of "bearing" with one another is learning to hear God speak through difficult people.[162]

Bruce L. Bugbee, founder and president of Network Ministries

[158] John Ortberg, *The Life you've always wanted* (Grand Rapids, Michigan: Zondervan, 1997), 99.

[159] John Ortberg, *The Life you've always wanted*, 99-100.

[160] John Ortberg, 100-101.

[161] John Ortberg, 102-103.

[162] Ibid., 116.

International, and Don Cousins, founder and president of Team Development Inc., point out the difference between servanthood and servility. Servanthood is serving with love. Servility is without love. Servanthood serves out of "I want to serve God," while servility serves out of "I *have* to serve God." Servanthood is motivated by "what God sees" as to serve an audience of One, while servility is motivated by "what others see" as to serve to please others. Furthermore, servanthood has an attitude of "whatever it takes" as effort may exceed expectations, while servility has attitude of "it is not my job" as it performs the minimum. Finally, servanthood's results are "God-glorifying" as it directs attention to God humbly reflecting Christ, while servility's result is "self-seeking" as it draws attention to self, pridefully promoting self.[163] Always keeping in mind that Christian ministers are called to serve and are called to suffer for Jesus Christ will help a minister maintain his or her focus as a suffering servant of God.

We have a false understanding of our role as Christian ministers. We think, and others expect that we are capable of fixing all problems and knowing all answers. Existing in a "superman" culture, reinforces what we think about ourselves. In truth, only God is the fixer/healer; we are but the instruments, as vulnerable as any we serve.

"We have this treasure in jars of clay to show that this all-surpassing power is from God and not from us." (2 Corinthians 4:7 NIV) We are as vulnerable and breakable as "jars of clay." We are called to serve as suffering servants as Jesus Christ was. We are not to compare ourselves with others as the church of Corinth compared Paul with Peter and Apollo. It is the responsibility of a Christian minister to be on guard against conforming to the worldly expectations of a mass media-saturated society or well-established ministry.

Dr. Douglas Groothuis, professor of philosophy at Denver

---

[163] Bruce Bugbee and Don Cousins., *Network Participant's guide* (Grand Rapids, Michigan: Zondervan, 2005), 102.

Seminary, points out that "apologetics [church leaders] are limited not only by the difficulty of the subject [ministry] itself, but by the weakness of the subjects who practice it—us [pastors, missionaries, leaders]. . . . We are sinners. . . . We are the medium for this matchless message, but we are flawed. . . . We may study too much and pray too little, or the opposite."[164] (Bracketed words are added by the author.)

Throughout his years of ministry, Paul developed a deep sense of who he was: "Christ Jesus came into the world to save sinners, of whom I am the foremost," (I Timothy 1:15b, ESV), along with a theme for his compatibility with ministry: "Who is weak, and I do not feel weak? Who is led into sin, and I do not inwardly burn?" (2 Cor. 11:29, NIV.)

Reflecting on who we are and how we are called to serve, and to suffer as God's servants, will leave us standing firm between the Great Shepherd and the sheep for which we are held accountable.

[164] Douglas Groothuis., *Christian Apologetics :A Comprehensive Case for Biblical Faith* (Downers Grove, IL: Inter-varsity Press, 2011), 71.

5

From Lack of a Personal Confidant to Having a Personal Confidant

Lack of a Personal Confidant

Lack of a personal confidant has been identified as a contributor to the emotional exhaustion of burnout.[165] "A confidant is . . . someone who has earned one's confidence, and it is only to such trusted or trustworthy individuals that full disclosure is made."[166] We even find evidence in the life of Jesus of his need for a personal confidant to support him, but the only unfailing support he received in times of crisis was from the Father. After the Last Supper, Jesus asked his disciples—especially his core group, Peter, James and John—to accompany him to Gethsemane (Matt. 26: 26-46). Yet his earthly confidants left him, out of their fear of being caught, even when they did not intend to betray him. Thus,

---

[165] Susan Jackson, Michael P. Leiter, and Christina Maslach, *Maslach Burnout Inventory Manual* (Palo Alto, CA: Consulting Psychologists, 1996), 37.

[166] John Fitzgerald, "Christian Friendship: John, Paul, and the Philippians," *Interpretation* 61, no. 3 (2007): 284-96, 285, New Testament Abstracts, EBSCOhost (November 15, 2010).

It is grace (John 1:17) rather than demonstrated merit and reliability on the disciples' part that creates friendship between Jesus and his disciples. By treating his followers as friends, Jesus makes them precisely that. The disciples' continuing friendship with Jesus depends on their willingness to follow his instructions (John 15:14), just as Jesus himself has kept the Father's commandments and thus has abided in his love (John 15:10).[167]

In his most agonizing moment after "an angel appeared to him from heaven, strengthening him," Jesus only "prayed more earnestly; and his sweat became like great drops of blood falling down to the ground." (Luke 22:43-44 NIV) At that moment, God the Father was his only reliable confidant. Therefore, in Jesus's experience, disciples, human confidants, were important but not as much as the only faithful and powerful personal confidant, God the Father.

Paul also knew the importance of personal confidants. He was especially blessed with spiritual prayer and material support from his friendship with the church of Philippi.

> The Philippians . . . continued to share their possessions with Paul as an expression of their fellowship. Paul has received from Epaphroditus the gifts they have now sent to him in prison (4:10-13), and he prays that God will likewise reward them: "My God will supply every need of yours according to his riches in glory in Christ Jesus." (Phil 4:18-19 ESV)[168]

This church decreased Paul's emotional exhaustion, for they shared not only the same love (Phil. 2:2), but were also "going

---

[167] Ibid.
[168] Johnson, "Making Connections: The Material Expression of Friendship in the New Testament," *Interpretation* 58, no. 2 (2004): 158, New Testament Abstracts, EBSCOhost (November 15, 2010).

through the same struggle you saw I had." (Phil. 1:30 NIV)[169] "Paul's emphasis on sharing something in common and engaging in mutual enterprises is [reflected in] his use of the koinos [informal Greek] language." (syn: Phil 1:7, 27; 2:17-18, 25; 3:10, 17; 4:3, 14.)[170]

Individually, he treasured his "true yokefellow. …. laboured with me in the gospel," (Phil. 4:3 ERV), and especially Timothy as a person "of one soul, one spirit, and one mind" with whom he could share friendship (Phil. 1:27; 2:20). It is understandable, then, that Paul asked for Timothy to be with him near the end of his life (2 Tim. 1:16-18; 4:17). Throughout Paul's life, he would "sow bountifully" (2 Cor. 9:6) in the lives of "fellow-laborers" such as Barnabas (Acts 13:1), Mark (Acts 13:5; 2 Tim. 4:11), Silas (Acts 15:40), Luke, Lydia (Acts 16:13-15, 40), Aquila and Priscilla (Acts 18:1-5), Titus (Titus 1:4) and Epaphras (Col. 4:12).

But even when surrounded by a large group of personal confidants, Paul always held God as his only faithful, powerful friend: . . . "persecuted, but not abandoned; struck down, but not destroyed. We always carry around in our body the death of Jesus, so that the life of Jesus may also be revealed in our body." (2 Cor. 4:9, 10,NIV) "That Paul was still strong whenever he was weak (2 Cor. 12:10) was due to God's friendship with him."[171] At the end of his life and ministry, no one came to see him, "But the Lord stood by me and strengthened me." (2 Tim. 4:16-17,NIV) In this moment of helplessness, Paul's reliance solely on the Lord's appearance parallels the time before His Crucifixion when Jesus Christ derived strength from the angel.

Pastors need support systems to help reestablish priorities, regain perspective, and find refuge in times of trouble. Finding real friendship can be complicated, depending on how pastors view themselves. When pastors view themselves exclusively in terms of

---

[169] Ibid., 294.
[170] Ibid.
[171] Ibid., 296.

their vocation, it puts relational distance between the pastor and the congregation. And lonely pastors find it difficult to separate themselves mentally from their roles as spiritual guides. Charles Haddon Spurgeon addresses the pastor's dilemma:

> A minister fully equipped for his work will usually be a spirit by himself, above, beyond, and apart from others. The most loving of his people cannot enter into his peculiar thoughts, cares, and temptations. In the ranks, men walk shoulder to shoulder, with many comrades, but as the officer rises in rank, men of his standing are fewer in number. There are many soldiers, few captains, fewer colonels, but only one commander-in-chief. So, in our churches, the man whom the Lord raises as a leader becomes, in the same degree in which he is a superior man, a solitary man. The mountaintops stand solemnly apart, and talk only with God as He visits their terrible solitudes.[172]

Swiss psychiatrist Carl Jung, largely credited as the founder of analytical psychology, suggests that pastors wear psychological masks over their real inner feelings when they relate to others.[173] While pastors need to remain "professional," sooner or later the pastoral role becomes "maladaptive."[174] They strive to fulfill the role of pastor without allowing others to touch their real self. Pastors in this situation are on a path toward burnout syndrome and tend

---

[172] C. H. Spurgeon, *Lectures to My Students* (Grand Rapids, MI: Zondervan, 1980), 157.

[173] Murray Stein, *Jung's Treatment of Christianity* (Wilmette, IL: Chiron, 1985), 139-46.

[174] William H. Willimon, *Clergy and Laity Burnout* (Nashville, TN: Abingdon, 1989), 38.

to drop out as they face progressively overwhelming needs and demands.

One case study describes a pastor who was called to a downtown Chinese church. The congregation expected him to live close to them, but the pastor and his family chose to live in the suburbs and commute. The members held expectations of the pastor's wife and children that the family was not willing to assume. Some church members were unhappy with this.[175] Such factors affect the pastor's long-term effectiveness, a problem heightened by the lack of friends or a strong support system.

In response to this author's survey, pastors described difficulty in finding people to talk with about personal issues. Responses included: "I don't have any friends." "I do not have enough time for friends." "I am a pastor. I know what the congregation expects from me. It is very difficult to talk with them. Few of my seminary classmates with whom I graduated stayed in the same town."[176] Since these pastors are susceptible to burnout, the cultural and institutional dynamics that contribute to mental, spiritual, and emotional exhaustion must be evaluated.

The importance of friends and support might be even more crucial to a pastor's vocational success and personal health than it is to those outside full-time ministry. A 1976 study of clergy members reported: "It seems that stress was hardest to resolve when external support was absent. This was particularly true when the source of stress was in marriage or family."[177] Comparing the 2006 Barna Group survey on Protestant pastors' personal relationships with Paul Wright's work on pastors' friendships published in 1985, parishioners tended to be quite parochial about their pastors and would disapprove if they developed friendships that were overly

---

[175] Yuan, responses to "4-Out" Questionnaire (November, 2006).

[176] Ibid.

[177] Barbara G. Gilbert, *Who Ministers to Ministers?* (New York: Alban Institute, 1976), 21.

exclusive or "special."[178] Sixty-one percent of the pastors in the United States lost their sense of connection with others.[179] This reveals how easy it is for the pastor to suffer from burnout without a confidant.

When pastors have few friends or no friends at all, it is not entirely due to their perceived ministry roles. It also reflects a prevailing culture that values individualism, intelligence and self-sacrifice. Robert Bellah (et al) describes the archetypal American hero with which the American pastor must contend:

> America is the inventor of that most mythic hero, the cowboy, who again and again saves a society he can never completely fit into. The cowboy has a special talent—he can shoot faster and straighter than most other men—and a special sense of justice. But these characteristics make him so unique that he can never fully belong to society. It is as if the myth says you can be a truly good person, worthy of admiration and love, only if you resist fully joining the group. . . . The connection of moral courage and lonely individualism is even more evident for that other more modern American hero, the hard-boiled detective. From Sam Spade to Serpico, the detective is a loner. He is often unsuccessful in conventional terms, working out of a shabby office where the phone never rings. But his marginality is also his strength. When the detective begins his quest, it appears to be an isolated incident, but as it develops, the case turns out to be linked to the powerful and

---

[178] See text associated with above notes 37, 38; and Tegan Blackbird and Paul Wright, "Pastor's Friendship, Part I: Project Overview and Expectation of the Pedestal Effect," *Journal of Psychology and Theology* 13, no. 4 (Winter 1988): 274.

[179] Blackbird and Wright, ibid.

privileged of the community. Society, particularly "high society," is corrupt to the core. To seek justice in a corrupt society, the American detective must be tough and, above all, he must be a loner.

Both the cowboy and the hard-boiled detective tell us something important about American individualism. The cowboy, like the detective, can be valuable to society only because he is a completely autonomous individual who stands outside it. To serve society, one must be able to stand alone, not needing others, not depending on their opinions, and not submitting to their wishes. Yet this individualism is not selfishness. Indeed, it is a kind of heroic selflessness. One accepts the necessity of remaining alone in order to serve the values of the group. Yet it is part of the profound ambiguity of the mythology of American individualism that its moral heroism is always just a step away from despair.[180]

It should also be noticed that, due to constant vocational challenges, pastors need their *own* pastors. James Means suggests this relationship is essential for the pastor's health, although it may be contrary to the image of either an "American hero" or a "Hollywood Superman." Admitting, as a pastor, that one *needs* a pastor requires one to put away the self-image of "Super Leader." Pastors who hold their title as a position rather than a call to be a servant of God

---

[180] Robert Bellah, Richard Madsen, William M. Sullivan, Ann Swidler and Steven M. Tipton, *Habits of the Heart: Individualism and Commitment in American Life* (New York: Haperennial Library, 1985), 145-46.

have difficulty sharing things that may reflect negatively on their reputations as heroes.[181]

One interview conducted for this book involved a pastor who admitted he would stay in ministry *just* to provide a living for his family. An experienced pastor may be able to perform a ministerial routine without cultivating friendships or fresh challenges. A lack of personal confidants places pastors at even more serious risk of burnout symptoms, and they may eventually suffer the long-term devastation of dropping out.

Journey To Find a Personal Confidant

Before finding a personal confidant, it is wise to learn whether, as a Christian minister, one is qualified to be a personal confidant to another Christian minister. The journey starts from a deep, self-reflection process. This process will be permeated with key ingredients for Christian pilgrimage and spiritual warfare: love, faith, hope, truth and grace. This pilgrimage is intended to remove the masks of the Christian leader, to break through the individualism and to re-discover the relationship between Jesus and the disciples, and the bonding between Paul and Timothy, in the Christian community.

God is a God of relationship. We are God's children (John 1:12). We are God's friends (John 15:15). We are united with the Lord (1 Cor. 6:17). We are members of the body of Christ (1 Cor. 12:27). We are ministers of reconciliation for God (2 Cor. 5:17-21). We are God's co-workers (1 Cor. 3:9; 2 Cor. 6:1). We have been adopted as God's children (Eph. 1:5). We can love one another because God loves us first (1 John 4:19). Moreover, we do not merely experience love from the Triune God. We are also blessed by the loving community of grace in three persons. We all are spiritual friends, spiritual family members and spiritual confidants to each other. The visitations from

---

[181] James Means, *The Madness of Ministry* (Denver, CO: Denver Seminary, 1979), 12.

Chi Eng Yuan

God to Abraham (Gen. 18:1-15), incarnation of the Lord Jesus Christ (Luke 2:1-7), and the indwelling of Holy Spirit (2 Cor. 1:22) have revealed God's agenda for those whom He calls to serve, to practice His presence and to love one another.

Am I a faithful confidant in Christ? A good Christian minister confidant needs to know him or herself well, in order to help others. And knowing oneself deeply comes from a deep relationship with God.

The process of deepening one's relationship with God through deep repentance and true confession comes from facing personal insecurities and demons, admitting mistakes and failures, and learning from them. In his book *Why Are Christians Living Just Like the Rest of the World*, Ronald J. Sider points out that the problem that keeps the pastor away from God is the "pervasive individualism that devastates the Western Church."

As Gordon MacDonald details in his book *A Resilient Life*, repairing the past begins with repentance: "He had to stop and say, 'I'm lost.' That was followed by a search for the right way and then a retracing of steps until he was back on the right path." As Christian ministers, we must admit that we have pride, the foundation on which the dark side is built which is extremely destructive when left unchecked. It is an area that many Christian leaders ignore when it comes to accountability to others. In their book *Overcoming the Dark Side of Leadership*, Gary L. McIntosh and Samuel D. Rina Sr. help the reader understand how the *reality* (pridefully attempting to meet unrealistic expectations) causes conflicts due to selfish power seeking, self-deception because of sin, and spiritual dryness because of wrong motives. In order to seek deep healing and true confession, we should make daily time for repentance because we are as selfish as James and John, the disciples of Jesus Christ, who requested special consideration and recognition from Jesus.

We also have an inherent ability to deceive ourselves. Even Paul recognized that his heart could be deceitful: "I care very little if I am judged by you or by any human court; indeed, I do not even judge myself. My conscience is clear, but that does not make me innocent. It is the Lord who judges me." (I Cor. 4:3-4,NIV) Additionally, we should learn from solid religious leaders in the Bible (King David, for example) who experienced significant failure as the direct result of a dark side.

Repentance is a must for a 'burn for Christ' pastor. I believe that the duration of "a daily time of repentance" should be proportional to age (for example, 10 minutes at age 25, 20 minutes at age 35 and so forth). We can use McIntosh and Rina's book as material for five weekend retreats. The first activity in each retreat is discovering and acknowledging what the primary and/or secondary dark side is.

Weekend 1	Am I a compulsive pastor as was Moses, status conscious, looking for reassurance and approval from those in authority, trying to control activities and keep order? Such pastors are usually workaholics. At times they are excessively moralistic, conscientious and judgmental.
Weekend 2	Am I a narcissistic pastor as Solomon, driven to succeed by a need for admiration and acclaim? This pastor may have an over-inflated sense of importance as well as great ambitions and grandiose fantasies. Am I self-absorbed and uncertain due to deep feelings of inferiority? In addition, do I not enjoy my successes and am I dissatisfied with my life?
Weekend 3	Am I a paranoid pastor as Saul, suspicious, hostile, fearful, jealous, and afraid that someone will undermine my leadership? Am I hypersensitive to others' actions, do I attach subjective meanings to motives, and do I create rigid structures for control? Am I feeling strong insecurity and a lack of confidence?

Weekend 4	Am I a codependent leader as Samson, a peacemaker who covers up problems rather than facing them, in an effort to balance the group system? Am I very benevolent with a high tolerance for deviant behavior? Am I willing to take on more work so I do not have to tell anyone "no"? Do I react rather than act? In my heart, am I a repressed and frustrated person who has trouble giving full, honest expressions to emotions or problems?
Weekend 5	Am I a passive-aggressive leader as Jonah, stubborn, forgetful, and intentionally inefficient? Do I tend to complain, resist demands, procrastinate and dawdle as a means of controlling my environment and those around me? On occasion, do I exert control through the use of short outbursts of sadness or anger? In my heart, am I angry and bitter? Do I have a fear of success, since it will lead to higher expectations?

The second activity during each retreat finds the pastor examining the past with the attitude of asking for forgiveness from our heavenly Father.

After this soul-searching step—"who I am?"—, getting rid of the obstacles of our journey and navigating the minefield of Christian ministers' spiritual battle is the next step. The First obstacle is the misunderstanding that a personal confidant must be a perfect person. Stories from the Bible show that godly people have their records of "falling down." From David in the Old Testament to Apostle Peter in the New Testament, it cannot be denied that no one is perfect. Even confidants may sleep during the critical time when their spiritual friends need them most, such as when our Lord was praying in Gethsemane (Matt. 26:36). We all are sinners. We are forgiven by our Lord who continues to be our friend when we truly repent and confess. We are unqualified to be His confidant but by God's grace and the power of the Holy Spirit, we *become* a personal confidant in Christ, positionally and practically. The time and place to conquer this misconception is, as Jean Vanier, founder of I' Arche community, wrote in her book *Community and Growth*, "When we accept that we have weaknesses and flaws, that we have sinned against God and against our brothers and sisters, but that we are forgiven and can grow towards inner freedom and truer love. Then we can accept the weaknesses and flaws of others. They [other potential personal confidants] too are forgiven by God and are growing towards the freedom of love."[182]

The Second obstacle is the one-way spiritual direction relationship that often happens in the Christian community. "Who is the pastor for Christian ministers?" becomes a serious question that increases with the increasing incidence of burnout among American, Chinese, Korean and African-American ministers. In terms of developing the relationship between personal confidants, I want to borrow the two-way mentoring connection between a mentor and a mentoree from Paul D. Stanley and J. Robert Clinton, defined in their book *Connecting*. In this both-way transferring of insights, experiences, relationships, ups and downs in their spiritual and physical lives, they embrace and empower each other by "sharing each other's burden." (Galatians 6:2,NLT) This process will reduce the temptation to become "Mr. Emotional Dumpster" for one or both of them.

The third and very important session of this journey is the five-week series of steps toward finding personal confidants.

---

[182] Jean Vanier, *Community and Growth* (New York, Mahwah: Paulist, 1989).,35.

Week 1: Do I *need* a personal confidant?

Ask the question every day: *Do I need a personal confidant?* Then study the Bible to answer it. Christian ministers can study this topic in the Old Testament, from Moses, who listened to his father-in-law giving him a priceless answer that saved him from burnout, to David with his confidant, Jonathan, who risked his life because of this friendship. Later, one can study this issue in New Testament from our Lord Jesus to Apostle Paul.

Mid-week, pastors can study the "clouds of witness" in church history related to their mission fields, such as the friendship between John Newton and Wilberforce.

At week's end, ask yourself the following: Have I felt loneliness and withdrawal from people? Was I a loner by upbringing, family and/or church? Am I more capable than Jesus and Paul or other men or women of faith in Hebrews 11? How many confidants have I had or prayed to have? Confess to God and pray for His guidance.

Week 2: Thinking about a personal confidant

Think about your past. Try to recall friends, close relatives, or companions who were in the category of trustworthy individuals. Remember what happened to both of you and what is happening now.

Think about your present situation. On index cards, write the names of one or more of your present or potential future confidants. Pray to establish or renew accountable covenant relationships with them.

Think about your future. What might be your greatest joy in Christ resulting from your mutual confidant relationships in the next five years? Dream and pray for this. Do not listen to the negative, discouraging voices from your past or from others' stories who say they cannot find personal confidants or that it is too risky. Be brave and be courageous.

Week 3: Your story of a personal confidant

Write an informal, self-discovery account of your journey of making friends, some of whom became confidants. This journey should start from childhood. Our inner circle to our getting-acquainted circle may include our parents, siblings, classmates or neighbors. When we become Christians, our journey will include pastors, Sunday school teachers and friends in our church or churches. If we enter Bible School or seminary, our journey of friendship will include roommates, classmates and professors in those circumstances. Our lists will include co-workers in our careers, so we will write down the co-labourers in ministry throughout our years as church planners, missionaries, pastors or seminarians. If you are married, is your spouse your confidant?

Think about these personal confidants. What draws you to them as close friends? Think of the most pleasant, intimate relationships you've had. Where are they now? Remember, you are thinking of the good times from the past. Can you develop a new mutual mentor relationship in your new page of life? Can history of "wonderful time together" happen to you again? Bring your request to the throne of Grace and Mercy now.

Week 4: My personality as a personal confidant

Personal relationships with others gives us a big pool of potential personal confidants because we can know "the depths of the ugliness of each other's lives and yet see each other in love, in trust, and with the heart of a brother and a sister."[183]

We are serving in an American church culture that adapted individualism, in contrast with the early church model that sees our identity in a perspective of having a Triune God as our Father and

---

[183] Kyle Strobel, *Metamorpha* (Grand Rapids, Michigan:BakerBooks, 2007), 123.

enjoying the love from the community of Grace, Truth, Faith, Love and Hope.

Do a reflection from the *Cape Town Commitment*, Article 9, We Love the People of God: "The people of God are those from all ages and all nations whom God in Christ has loved, chosen, called, saved and sanctified as a people for his own possession, to share in the glory of Christ as citizens of the new creation. As those, then, whom God has loved from eternity to eternity and throughout all our turbulent and rebellious history, we are commanded to love one another. For 'since God so loved us, we also ought to love one another,' and thereby 'be imitators of God...and live a life of love, just as Christ loved us and gave himself up for us.' Love for one another in the family of God is not merely a desirable option but an inescapable command. Such love is the first evidence of obedience to the gospel, the necessary expression of our submission to Christ's Lordship, and a potent engine of world mission. Jesus calls all his disciples together to be one family among the nations, a reconciled fellowship in which all sinful barriers are broken down through his reconciling grace. This Church is a community of grace, obedience and love in the communion of the Holy Spirit, in which the glorious attributes of God and gracious characteristics of Christ are reflected and God's multicolored wisdom is displayed. As the most vivid present expression of the kingdom of God, the Church is the community of the reconciled who no longer live for themselves, but for the Savior who loved them and gave himself for them."

Different kinds of personalities complement each other. Introverted Richard O'Connor in his book *Happy at Last* shares that his "extraverted wife has helped me feel more at ease, and thus enjoy many social situations where I would ordinarily run home as quickly as possible."[184] Using the Myers-Briggs Type Indicator (MBTI) to identify differences between one's own and one's personal confidant's four preference scales—extraversion/introversion, sensing/intuition,

---

[184] Richard O' Connor, *Happy at last* (New York, N.Y.:St. Martin, 2008)., 227.

feeling/thinking, and judging/perceiving—will deepen their understanding of each other and will complement each other.

Week 5: Do I have or must I still *find* the right personal confidant(s)?

If a Christian minister is married, think about the relationship with one's spouse. Is he or she a personal, spiritual confidant? How are bright sides and dark sides disclosed and shared between both of them? Has a challenge or an obstacle occurred in the past five years? Will there be progress over the next five years? A couple can experience, as personal confidants for each other, an intimate spiritual friendship as Aelred of Rievaulx, author of *On Spiritual Friendship*, points out: "Only those do we call friends to whom we can fearlessly entrust our heart and all its secrets; those too, who in turn, are bound to us by the same law of faith and security."[185]

The process of finding a personal confidant, stepping into a confidant relationship, can be intentional and natural after significant prayer, just as Jesus prayed through the night before choosing the twelve disciples. But what qualifies them as "personal confidants"? They must be godly servants of God. A personal, spiritual confidant is one who will hold a Christian leader accountable, providing direction if needed, providing insight into ministerial issues, and encouraging a commitment to grow into a mature Christian leader called to serve and to suffer for the Lord.

In addition to the requirement for their vertical relationship with God, it is helpful to find out about their horizontal relationships with others. Areas for consideration include the relationships in their homes and in their workplaces. Do they experience full disclosure and transparency with their close relationships or friendships? Are they self-disclosing as Apostle Paul was when he was at the low point

---

[185] Aelred of Rievaulx, *On Spiritual Friendship* (Washington, D.C.: Consortium Press, 1974)., 56.

of his life in 2 Cor. 1:8-9 NIV: . . . "far beyond our ability to endure, so that we despaired even of life. Indeed, in our hearts we felt the sentence of death...?" Are they humble as Paul when he asked his "sheep" with humility to "put up with a little of my foolishness"? (2 Cor. 11:1 NIV) Are they preaching with vulnerability by "sharing that careful blend of humanness without false humility, victories sans pride, presenting an authentic picture of God's work in their life? And that's one of the most important roles a sermon can play. This vulnerability demonstrates the pastor's willingness to admit failures and the desire to improve them. It also sets a tone that allows other people to admit they need help, too."[186]

Thus age, life experience, ministerial experience, personality, faith tradition, denomination/non-denomination, role in the ministry, and commitment level as personal confidants are all to be considered. Moreover, Judith A. Schwanz recommends choosing wisely, proceeding cautiously and deliberately, taking your time and letting relationships grow slowly before choosing a personal spiritual confidant. This often allows hidden motives to rise to the surface.[187]

Tilden H. Edwards, director of the Shalem Institute for Spiritual Formation,[188] suggests that when Christian ministers feel uncomfortable at the start of a new personal confidant relationship, "unless you come to a fairly clear sense that the person is wrong for you, then I would suggest a trial period of a few months with the person to give you time to 'relax into' the relationship. This will help sort out how much of your ambivalence is due simply to the inner resistance you would have with anyone, given the nature of the task, and how much is inherent in the relationship."

Finding a personal confidant is a life-long process because there

---

[186] Marshall Shelley, *Helping People Who Don;t Want Help* (Waco; Word, 1986), 66.?James E. Means 211.

[187] Judith A. Schwanz, *Blessed Connections* (Herndon, Virginia:Alban, 2008)., 103.

[188] Tilden H. Edwards, *Spiritual Friend* (New York, Ramsey:Paulist Press, 1980)., 121.

are many unknown factors in a Christian minister's life. From deep-cleaning of one's dark side, to becoming a trustworthy confidant oneself, to seriously praying and intentionally searching for a reliable confidant on the receiving end, it is long journey that is worth traveling because this can become the hallmark of "finishing well" for a solider in Christ.

6

From Managed By the Conflict to Managing the Conflict

Due to Hellenistic influences, the conflict (agōn) noted in the NT epistles largely involves a contest or fight amid great strain.[189] Paul is an example of a pastor who labors with great strain on behalf of the church, though supported by prayer and a unified spirit. Conflict seems inevitable for Paul. The tension in 2 Corinthians seems tailor-made to qualify him as a perfect candidate for burnout. Yet, despite these stormy circumstances, Paul still writes in 2 Corinthians to "get the church back on track and away from apostolic competitors who do not have the church's best interest at heart."[190]

As one who loved the Corinthian church but experienced never-ending challenges and numerous attacks from the body of Christ, Paul was at obvious risk of emotional exhaustion and was tempted to withdraw from his attackers and evaluate himself negatively, particularly in light of his ministry to the Corinthian church.

---

[189] Cheryl A. Kirk-Duggan, "Conflict," in *The New Interpreter's Dictionary of the Bible*, ed. K. D. Sakenfeld, vol. 1 (Nashville, TN: Abingdon, 2006), 717.
[190] Linda L. Belleville, *2 Corinthians* (Downers Grove, IL: InterVarsity, 1996), 13.

It would be easy for him to feel unhappy about this ministry. As a pastor, Paul showed both paternal and maternal love towards the Corinthians; he spent three years serving them and was still dissatisfied with his accomplishments as an apostle. Burned out pastors always feel exhausted as a result of dealing with the conflicts of the churches they have founded or served.

There is evidence of Paul's emotional exhaustion due to his long suffering with the Corinthian church. As Belleville points out:

> Criticisms were being leveled against him on two fronts. First, the Corinthians were charging him with vacillation in arranging his travel plans— saying yes to paying them a return visit only to change his mind at a later point (2 Cor. 1:12-2:4). They also accused him of professional arrogance, while lacking appropriate credentials (2 Cor. 3:1-4:5).[191]

Conflict can easily arise from tension between a Christ-like pastor and a worldly church. The Corinthian church belonged to this latter category. Like first-century worshipers regardless of their religious affiliation, they wanted "health, wealth, protection and sustenance, not moral transformation." Where money and family connections meant little and where social location and status meant everything, "The materialism and self-serving individualism and status-oriented civil religion of the day, fueled by the self-glorifying entertainment and sports subculture, presented a formidable front for the gospel of the cross and for its cruciform messenger." (Cf. I Cor. 1: 17-19 with II Cor. 2:14-17.)[192]

Paul also came into conflict with those who viewed themselves as superior to others in the church, a common problem in today's

---

[191] Ibid., 19.

[192] Scott. J. Hafemann, *2 Corinthians*, NIV Application Commentary (Grand Rapids, MI: Zondervan, 2000), 26-27.

churches as well. The Corinthian believers apparently tolerated widespread arrogance in the body of Christ: "In fact, you even put up with anyone who enslaves you or exploits you or takes advantage of you or pushes himself forward or slaps you in the face." (2 Cor. 11:20 NIV) Moreover, Paul had to deal with false apostles, as the Corinthians not only revered these leaders at face value only, they permitted them to move into positions of influence and leadership and to take over the life of the community . . . The false apostles had exploited the congregation for a tidy sum. They pushed themselves forward so successfully that the local Corinthian leadership was intimidated, suffering bruising insults.[193]

Paul's experience of dealing with a variety of conflict was hardly a one-of-a-kind situation in the history of redemption and the 2000-year history of the Church. Paul's experience is all too typical of opposition to the coming Kingdom of God, the theme of the whole Bible.[194] Paul as a follower of Jesus Christ and shepherd for the Kingdom of God was bearing his cross, experiencing opposition and tension from all angles. "The very heart of their message [that of Jesus, Paul and John] is Christ and the cross."[195] Paul noted his sufferings, loss, shame and defeats in 2 Cor. 11:23b-29. These experiences, evidence of the conflicts that Paul encountered in his ministry, result in loss of well-being for pastors both in the early Church and in the contemporary Church.

D.A. Carson, Research Professor of New Testament at Trinity Evangelical Divinity School, thus aptly concludes, "It is almost as if the primary (if not the only) incontestable criterion of true apostleship is massive suffering in the service of Christ." (cf. I Cor. 4:9-13; 2 Cor: 4:7-12; 6:4-5.)[196] Paul journeyed through his conflicts

---

[193] D.A.Carson, *A Model of Christian Maturity* (Grand Rapids, MI: Baker, 1993), 119.

[194] Larry R. Helyer, *The Witness of Jesus, Paul, and John: an Exploration in Biblical Theology* (Downers Grove, IL: InterVarsity, 2008), 382.

[195] Ibid., 385.

[196] Carson, *A Model of Christian Maturity*, 125.

bearing the cultural shame of being put into prison frequently, being flogged (which was also painful) and, most severely, being beaten with rods in public. He suffered dangers due to conflict with both his countrymen and the Gentiles for the sake of sharing the Good News. Even more than all these deep wounds, his burnout was caused by the betrayal of false brothers, the Jewish leaders (2 Cor. 11:23b-29). It would have been hard enough for Paul if this had happened only in Corinth, but Paul was pouring his energy into many churches:

> Paul seems to view his concern for all the churches as the climax of his trials. The immensity of the pressures and sufferings already enumerated serve as a measure of the intensity of his care for fellow believers. Certainly if many other congregations had problems as serious as those in Galatia and Corinth, Paul must have poured staggering quantities of emotional and spiritual energy into the churches he loved so well. . . . Paul engages all his considerable intellectual and emotional power in his ministry to the whole church. Such an approach bears fruit; but it takes its toll in energy consumed by deep involvement with people.[197]

As previously noted, one of the factors predisposing burnout is conflict among people within the pastor's circle. The resulting emotional exhaustion can ultimately drive pastors out of ministry. Both 2 Corinthians 1 and Philippians 1 indicate Paul may have faced severe emotional exhaustion, but it did not lead him to withdraw from ministry as most burnout victims do, nor did it rob him of a sense of personal achievement that might weaken his resolve to serve the Lord. Murray Harris notes that Paul "had recently experienced some unspecified affliction in the province of Asia that caused

---

[197] Ibid., 131-32.

him to be so utterly and unbearably crushed that he was forced to renounce all hope of survival." (2 Cor. 1:8.)[198] Paul was distracted by harsh criticism that he lacked resolve and integrity (1:17-22), was "inadequate" in ministry (cf. 2:16; 3:5-6), was self-promoting (3:1; 4:2), was "inferior" to the newly arrived Jewish missionaries (10:12-12:13), and declined their financial support (4:2).[199] This could be classified as emotional exhaustion, but the difference is that God intervened to deliver him, which re-energized him to continue ministry (1:10-11). Though God does not always rescue Paul, He comforts him through various kinds of suffering that in turn bring him future glory as his "sense of achievement." (4:16-17.)[200]

While imprisonment and persecution did not cause Paul to burn out, he was very concerned that "the Philippians are in a life-and-death struggle for the gospel in Philippi, and if their present unrest goes uncorrected, it could . . . blunt, if not destroy, their witness to Christ in their city."[201] As a pastor, Paul was concerned whether the Philippian church would endure the local growing harassment by the Roman officials.[202] Peter O'Brien adds that Paul's "two important issues are 'standing firm' and 'being united,' and these are expressions of living together as citizens worthy of the gospel of Christ."[203]

In short, even when ministry does not produce every burnout symptom, it can still die due to emotional exhaustion of the pastor unless God intervenes to provide deliverance, which he did for Paul. Moreover, the accumulated concerns of "routine" pastoral care can definitely cause emotional exhaustion, such as Paul's daily pressure of anxiety for all churches. "Who is weak, and I do not feel weak?

---

[198] Murray Harris, *The Second Epistle to the Corinthians* (Grand Rapids, MI: Eerdmans, 2005), 123.

[199] Barnett, *Second Epistle to the Corinthians*, 42.

[200] Harris, *Second Epistle to the Corinthians*, 123.

[201] Fee, *Philippians*, 32.

[202] Ibid.

[203] O'Brien, *Philippians*, 36.

Who is led into sin, and I do not inwardly burn?"(2 Cor. 11:28-29, NIV) Paul was later able to recharge, but only with God's power.

Moreover, Paul "burns when he sees righteousness in ruins and believers morally battered by the servants of Satan."[204] Paul does not just take the heat of "shame" from the culture of his time and the churches in which he ministered, but also burns inwardly at the weakness and shame of those false apostles. Paul also boasted of his own weakness (2 Cor. 11:30-33), a dramatic contrast to the "self-praise" of his society as well as that of ours today.[205] Kar Yong Lim explains that:

> As Paul's list of hardships demonstrates, this experience of suffering is not what a physically weak person would have been able to endure. It is also significant . . . that embedded in the notion of weakness are negative social connotations. Weakness is not merely what one senses himself, it is evaluated by others to be humiliating (cf. 2 Cor. 10:10; 11:21).[206]

Paul had great potential for burnout; the 26 kinds of suffering he listed would be expected to cause him severe emotional exhaustion and lack of any sense of accomplishment. But for Paul, what appeared on the surface to be a loss of harmony actually brought a resolution of his conflict. "Suffering and weakness is the vehicle for the mediation and embodiment of the gospel and the character of the crucified Christ, despite its negative social connotations."[207] Indeed, Paul's most trying yet his most edifying experience was the thorn in his flesh. Barnett comments on 2 Corinthians 12:7-10: "Broadly speaking, Paul's reference has been thought to be either [a] physical

---

[204] Carson, *A Model of Christian Maturity*, 133.

[205] Ibid., 135.

[206] Kar Yong Lim, *'The Sufferings of Christ Are Abundant in Us' (2 Corinthians 1:5)* (New York: T & T Clark, 2009), 173.

[207] Ibid., 180.

(an illness, disfigurement, or disability), [b] moral (temptation) or [c] relational (opposition to his ministry or persecution)."[208]

Paralleling Jesus's prayer during his last 24 hours of life in Gethsemane—which revealed God's power in the surrender of the powerless crucified Messiah—Paul exemplified in his own life how the Lord's resurrected power is "perfected in weakness, that is, in the weakness of the thorn that is not taken away."[209] The prayer of Christ is not limited in its benefit to Paul as an apostle but applies to whatever circumstances of life render us powerless, whether pastors or those in the flock. The one thing denied to us, which is exactly what most people demand above all, is control over our own destiny. For pastors to stay in the ministry rather than burn out or drop out, they are to "call out to the Lord not for resignation but for acceptance: active obedience to the Lord who, in response to our prayer, continues to say, 'My grace is sufficient for you, for my power is made perfect in weakness.' "[210]

Conflict in the ministry is inevitable. Stephen Muse found that conflict tends to impeach "the validity of their call to ministry, to take a toll on their personal sense of self-worth and family well-being leaving ministry."[211] The conflict involves denomination officials (26 percent), multiple demands (12 percent), needs of family and children (11 percent), church members (9 percent), senior pastors (8 percent), and church staff."[212]

Archibald Hart cites a study conducted by Fuller Theological Seminary in the late 1980s, which revealed that "40 percent [of ministers] reported at least one serious conflict with at least one parishioner at least once a month."[213] Likewise, this author's previous survey reveals that among pastors of the Association of North America Chinese Evangelical

---

[208] Barnett, *Second Epistle to the Corinthians*, 569.

[209] Ibid., 572-73.

[210] Ibid., 574.

[211] Stephen Muse, "Clergy in Crisis: When Human Power Isn't Enough," *The Journal of Pastoral Care & Counseling* 61, no. 3 (Fall 2007): 183.

[212] Hoge and Wenger, *Pastor in Transition*, 135.

[213] Hart, "Fuller Seminary Study."

Free Churches, 21 percent report conflict because of congregational politics or powerful individuals.[214] Similarly, a 2007 report on English speaking Chinese churches and their leaders suggests that one of the main reasons pastors leave the ministry of their English-speaking congregations is "conflict with people." The survey also provides some insightful suggestions for leadership and conflict management:

> My experience with my interns and my observation of most difficulties experienced by my pastoral friends has to do with having conflict with different people. There's a tendency to "externalize" and blame the problem on the board, our senior pastor, the immature congregants. . . .But there's a lack of self-examination in these cases. I believe that while it is true that other people contribute to the conflict, it is also true that with the proper training in how to relate to our superiors, such as senior pastor and board members, our co-workers and our flock, many of the conflicts could be anticipated, avoided or resolved before they become irreparable.[215]

Douglas G. McKown's research leads him to conclude that an increase in conflict may result in burnout and push the pastor toward dropout.[216] Moreover, the survey shows that a number of pastors are forced out as a direct result of conflict between themselves and powerful leaders or between the senior pastor and other pastoral staff.

---

[214] Chi Eng Yuan, Questionnaire.

[215] "Chinese Coordinative Centre of World Evangelism English Task Force Survey Summary Report—English Speaking Chinese Churches and Their Leaders" (April 2007, CCCOWE), 4-5, available at www.ccowe.org/eng (accessed August 29, 2007).

[216] Douglas G. McKown, "Pastors in Conflict: the Nature, Extent, Contributing Factors and Consequences of Conflict in Ministry" (Ph.D. diss., Fuller Theological Seminary, 2001), 82.

Melvin Wong discusses the pitfalls of poor conflict-resolution skills, which can be traced to past wounds and may lead some pastors to choose avoidance or "cut-and-run":

> Avoidance is denial and the overly simplistic belief of "time heals" and a "let the past be in the past" strategy in solving problems. Instead of focusing on the issue of resolving the conflict, the unhealthy pastor will focus on the perceived offender and attempt to discredit him by backbiting and manipulation.[217]

In light of such inevitable conflict, Gambill and Lineberger observe that:

> Whether during times of conflict or harmony, the majority of ministry is set within an emotional context. Knowing how to perceive and use emotion (i.e., having emotional intelligence) has a huge impact on an individual's ability to form and maintain effective relationships. . . . Emotional intelligence is crucial to good leadership.[218]

In short, conflict is an area for pastors to address proactively with wisdom and maturity if they are to avoid burnout and eventual dropout. An evaluation of the research and literature on pastoral burnout suggests evidence of interpersonal factors such as lack of confidants, poor conflict management and cultural clash, along with individual factors such as incompatibility, insufficient rest and, most important, spirituality, a right relationship with God.

---

[217] Melvin W. Wong, "A Psychologically Healthy Pastor" (Christian Mental Health, July 19, 2001), available at http://www.christianmentalheanlth.com/pastor.html (accessed Dec 10, 2010).

[218] Chris Gambill and Molly Linberger, "Emotional Intelligence and Effective Conflict Management," *Congregations* (Fall 2009): 28.

Journey to manage the conflict

The journey begins with an admission of reality in the body of Christ, especially if one is a pastor. Frederick Buechner, in his book *Whistling in the Dark: A Doubter's Dictionary*, suggests that the church is like Noah's Ark:

"The nave is the central part of the church from the main front to the chancel. It's the part where the laity sit and in great Gothic churches is sometimes separated from the choir and clergy by a screen. It takes its name from the Latin navis, meaning ship, one reason being that the vaulted roof looks rather like an inverted keel. A more interesting reason is that the Church itself is thought of as a ship or Noah's Ark. It's a resemblance worth thinking about.

"In one as in the other, just about everything imaginable is aboard, the clean and the unclean both. They are all piled in together helter-skelter, the predators and the prey, the wild and the tame, the sleek and beautiful ones and the ones that are ugly as sin. There are sly young foxes and impossible old cows. There are the catty and the piggish and the peacock-proud. There are hawks and there are doves. Some are wise as owls, some silly as geese; some meek as lambs and others fire-breathing dragons. There are times when they all cackle and grunt and roar and sing together, and there are times when you could hear a pin drop. Most of them have no clear idea just where they're supposed to be heading or how they're supposed to get there or what they'll find if and when they finally do, but they figure the people in charge must know and in the meanwhile sit back on their haunches and try to enjoy the ride.

"It's not all enjoyable. There's backbiting just like everywhere else. There's a pecking order. There's jostling at the trough. There's growling and grousing, bitching and whining. There are dogs in the manger and old goats and black widows. It's a regular menagerie in there, and sometimes it smells to high Heaven like one.

"But even at its worst, there's at least one thing that makes it bearable within, and that is the storm without—the wild winds and terrible waves and in all the watery waste, no help in sight. And at its best there is, if never clear sailing, shelter from the blast, a sense of somehow heading in the right direction in spite of everything, a ship to keep afloat and, like a beacon in the dark, the hope of finding safe harbor at last."

The journey's second leg is to clarify the meaning of conflict management:

Conflict is interaction among parties who are interdependent and who believe that the other parties in the conflict intend to prevent them from achieving their goals or having their needs met. It is important to recognize that conflicts can be driven by perceptions, and not merely by the objective situation. Interdependence plays a critical role in conflict because it sets up tendencies to compete or cooperate that drive conflict interaction.[219]

"Effective conflict management distinguishes two phases in a well-managed conflict: a differentiation phase and an integration phase. When differentiation is handled effectively, parties are able to express their positions and emotions. At the end of effective differentiation, parties have come to understand others' positions (though they might not agree with them), to recognize the legitimacy of others, and to have motivation to resolve the conflict. During effective integration, parties explore a range of solutions, develop a solution that meets the needs of all, and work out means of implementing the resolution."[220]

There are different basic styles of conflict management, which represent how people in organizations can relate to each other during conflict. Conflict styles represent basic patterns of behavior that people tend to enact during conflicts. Five styles, which differ in terms of their concern with satisfying one's own goals and their concern for others' goals, can be distinguished: competing, accommodating, avoiding, collaborating and compromising.[221] From the University of Maryland, animal analogies of these five styles are described as below:

---

[219] Joseph P. Folger, Marshall S. Poole and Randall K. Stutman, *Working Through Conflict* (New York:Longman, 2001)., 14.

[220] Ibid., 34.

[221] Ibid., 110.

Conflict Management Styles

<u>OWL</u> (Collaborating): I win, you win
Owls highly value their own goals and relationships. They view conflict as a problem to be solved and to seek a solution that achieves both their goals and the goals of the other person. Owls see conflicts as a means of improving relationships by reducing tensions between two persons. They try to begin a discussion that identifies the conflict as a problem. By seeking solutions that satisfy both themselves and the other person, owls maintain the relationship. Owls are not satisfied until a solution is found that achieves their goals and the other person's goals. They are not satisfied until the tensions and negative feelings have fully resolved.

<u>Turtle</u> (Avoiding): You bend, I bend

Turtles withdraw into their shells to avoid conflicts. They give up their goals and relationships, they stay away from the issues over which the conflict is taking place and from the persons they are in conflict with. Turtles believe it is easier to withdraw from a conflict than to face it.

Shark (Competing): **I win, you lose**

Sharks try to overpower opponents by forcing them to accept their solution to the conflict. Their goals are highly important to them, and relationships are of minor importance. They seek to achieve their goals at all costs. They are not concerned with the needs of others and do not care if others like or accept them. Sharks assume that conflicts are settled by one person winning and one person losing. They want to be a winner. Winning gives sharks a sense of pride and achievement. Losing gives them a sense of weakness, inadequacy and failure. They try to win by attaching, overpowering, overwhelming, and intimidating.

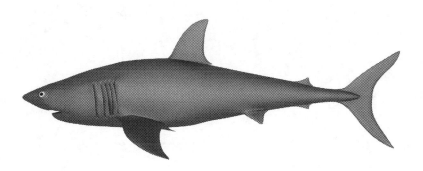

Teddy Bear (**Accommodating**): **I lose, you win**

To Teddy Bears, the relationship is of great importance while their own goals are of little importance. Teddy Bears want to be accepted and liked by others. They think that conflict should be avoided in favor of harmony and that people cannot discuss conflicts without damaging relationships. They are afraid that if the conflict continues, someone will get hurt and that would ruin the relationship. Teddy Bears say "I'll give up my goals and let you have what you want, in order for you to like me." Teddy Bears try to smooth over the conflict out of fear of harming the relationship.

Fox (Compromising): You bend, I bend

Foxes are moderately concerned with their own goals and their relationship with others. Foxes seek a compromise; they give up part of their goals and persuade the other person in a conflict to give up part of their goals. They seek a conflict solution in which both sides gain something; the middle ground between two extreme positions. They are willing to sacrifice part of their goals and relationships in order to find agreement for the common good.

"Power is the ability to influence or control events. It depends on resources parties can employ to influence others and attain their goals. A wide variety of resources may serve as sources of power, including material resources (money or strength), skills, likability and formal position in a group or organization."[222] Power is also the architecture of conflict interaction. The moves and countermoves in a conflict are based on parties' ability and willingness to use power. Power moves are based on resources people hold that serve as a successful basis of influence."[223]

"Face is a communicator's claim to be seen as a certain type of

---

[222] Ibid., 152.
[223] Ibid., 154.

person, the positive social value a person claims for him or herself."[224] "People lose face when their identity claims are challenged or ignored by others. Mutual acknowledgement and cooperative maintenance of face is one of the major concerns in everyday interaction."[225]

Is a person's style an unchanging characteristic? "People develop habitual styles that they tend to employ as their first tendency in conflicts. If we become award of our conflict styles, it is possible to change them and even to choose them strategically."[226]

How do I select an appropriate style? "How effective is the style likely to be in the situation? What responses will this style provoke? What will the consequences of the style be for long-term relationships among parties? Is the style ethical under the current conditions?"[227]

"Climate captures the overall feel of the situation for parties. It is experienced in common by members of a group or dyad, and is a product of their interaction."[228]

"Reflective Thinking is designed to help parties avoid potential problems by tightly structuring discussion so that they do not consider solutions until they have understood the problem. It also encourages parties to explore a range of options when considering resolutions to the conflict and to evaluate each option thoroughly."[229]

"Reframing occurs when parties reinterpret the situation in a new light. This reframing alters how they orient to the conflict and their actions and reactions toward others."[230]

The third stop on our journey is to understand the level of conflict. Speed Leas, co-author (with Edward G. Dobson and Marshall Shelley) of *Mastering Conflict & Controversy*, points out that "the level of conflict has less to do with the problem than with

[224] Ibid., 182.
[225] Ibid., 183.
[226] Ibid., 267.
[227] Ibid., 268.
[228] Ibid., 216.
[229] Ibid., 280.
[230] Ibid., 281.

people's reaction to it. Just because we are open and honest with each other doesn't mean that real differences do not exist. Of course, as the stakes get higher, so does the possibility of more intense conflict."[231] The authors describe five levels of conflict:

- **Level-I** conflict involves predicaments, in which the major objective of the parties is to solve the problem;
- **Level-II**, disagreement, sees the objectives of the parties having shifted slightly; each party becomes increasingly concerned about self-protection;
- **Level-III** describes a contest where the "players" are less concerned about the problem or looking good; now they want to win, to get their way;
- **Level-IV**, a fight/flight response to conflict, reveals that the major objective of the parties is to break the relationship, either leaving or getting the other to withdraw.
- **Level-V**, intractable conflict, has parties willing to let the other side live, if at a distance. At Level V, the parties believe their opposition so evil and virulent that simply getting rid of them will not do.[232]

Leas also points out the 10 most predictable times of conflict in a church environment:

- Easter season
- stewardship campaigns/budget time
- addition of new staff
- change in leadership style
- the pastor's vacation
- changes in the pastor's family
- introduction of baby boomers into the church
- the completion of a new building

---

[231] Edward G. Dobson, Speed B. Leas and Marshall Shelley, 83.
[232] Ibid., 85-93.

- loss of church membership, and
- increase in church membership.[233]

The fourth stop on our journey of conflict management is to practice speaking the truth tempered by love. This can be developed into the material of a spiritual retreat for Christian ministers, based on Eph. 4:14-16: *A mature and growing faith, evidenced by truth and love.*

Jeff Rosenau asked the question in his book *When Christians act like Christians*: "If I communicate with someone who has an opposing view, is my desire to be 'right' or to do what is right for God's glory?"[234] A deeper examination of Eph. 4:14-16 reveals that "truth" means the truth of love/faithfulness. A truthful person is one who lives out his or her covenant obligations, which include both what is said and what is done. Living the truth in love is both the means of growth and the result of growth. Truth and love are wrapped together. Love rejoices with the truth (I Cor. 13:6). Accordingly, Christian ministers should speak the truth with love. The gospel is the word of truth, we are to speak and do the truth, and we are to worship in truth. Worship is telling the truth about God. Confession is telling the truth about ourselves.

The gospel expresses reality but rejects pseudo-reality. In other words, living the truth with love is personal, practical and all-embracing. Indeed, our God is a God of relationship. Our relationships with Him and with others are more important than issues. This practice will help us to speak honestly about fears, frustrations, angers, forgiveness and hopes, essential to knowing ourselves before handling relational issues. We also will find that speaking in love and hearing others speak to us in love is to enter into others' lives, to understand their struggles, to feel their pain. Throughout the process, we will realize that conflicts are divine-made opportunities for Christian ministers to grow in Him.

---

[233] Ibid., 109-116.
[234] Jeff Rosenau, *When Christians act like Christians* (Centennial, Colorado:Accountability, 2010), 38.

In the spirit of speaking the truth in love, rooting out causes of conflict is the basis for managing them. Three human shortcomings that cause church conflict include *fear* of what is happening (or not happening) in the church after anxiety turns into worry; *needs* in conflict with the *needs* of others; and sins. Issues of solving the problems can be resolved with the steps as listed below:

- clearly define the problem
- agree on the problem's definition
- explore alternative solutions.
- develop criteria for selecting one of the alternatives either by collaboration or by negotiation.[235]

Moreover, "When faced with value differences, the church has a few options:

- reframe the problem
- partition, meaning to ensure that the disputing parties do not share the same space at the same time
- agree not to deal with the issue."[236]

Kirk Blackard and James W. Gibson emphasized in their book *Capitalizing on Conflict* that . . ."when only the symptoms of a conflict are addressed, the learning isn't embedded in the organization, and people thus do the same things time and again. The process for addressing root causes will depend on the circumstances . . . experience, intuition, and deciding what "why" questions to ask in arriving at an answer. Once the underlying whys are discovered, however, this information can be objectively assessed as part of the decision process addressing what to do systemically to reduce future conflict."[237]

---

[235] Marshall Shelley, ed. *Leading your church Through conflict and Reconciliation* (Minneapolis, Minnesota:Bethany, 1997), 104-107

[236] Ibid., 108-111

[237] Kirk Blackard and James W. Gibson, *Capitalizing on Conflict* (Palo Alto, California:David - Black, 2002)., 254-255.

As the final step of this learning process, bear in mind that no one in the church is the same. We are each unique in the eyes of God. In terms of the pace of any conflict resolution, taking time with a careful, slow pace will lead to better results. Throughout the process of making peace, it is wise to deal with one issue at a time rather than dealing with all problems at once. Be mindful of different perspectives that include cultural differences, personality differences, age differences, different up-bringings and so on, keeping track of all kinds of solutions to the problem(s).

Moreover, for those who are solving issues together, thinking through and making the best decision among various suggested solutions is a key process. Simultaneously, defining *inappropriate* conflict management is also recommended. Speed Leas (quoted above), a director of consultation for the Alban Institute, suggests that inappropriate conflict management includes name calling, mind reading (attributing evil motives to others), inducing guilt ("Look how you've made me feel!"), rejecting, deprecating/discrediting another person, using information from confidential sources, or even simply indicating that such information exists."[238]

John W. Frye emphasizes in his book *Jesus the Pastor* that . . . "empowered pastors accept spiritual conflict as a way of life."[239] That is, life is not necessarily a peaceful journey. It is also a life of spiritual battles. Conflicts are inevitable but actually are instruments from God to mold His children into the material of Christian ministers. However, "Pastors must make clear to each child of God, each member on the team, the individual nature of spiritual warfare— that is, the real and deadly conflict, and equip and coach each individual believer in skills to win the match."[240]

---

[238] Edward G. Dobson, Speed B. Leas and Marshall Shelley, *Mastering Conflict & Controversy* (Portland, Oregon:Multonmah,1992)., 44.

[239] John W. Frye, *Jesus the Pastor*(Grand Rapids, Michigan:Zondervan, 2000)., 132.

[240] Ibid., 126.

From Shocked by Culture to Managing Culture Shock

Cultural Clash

While workplace culture contributed to the effectiveness of participants in the author's study, it also highlighted one of the main components of burnout: unrealistic expectations based on culture. The term "culture" refers to material substance, norms of behaviors, values, beliefs, and expressive symbols or representations:

> ["Culture"] is broadly used to refer to the ways of life that offer systems for explaining meaning in the life-world of human society. . . . Culture, like theology (the interpretive meaning of God), is intertwined in the meaning of a life-world, and therefore plays a significant role in biblical interpretation. Theology can be part of a culture; culture can be a part of theology.[241]

---

[241] Khiok-Khong Yeo, "Cultural Study," in *New Interpreter's Dictionary of the Bible*, vol. 1, ed. K. D. Sakenfeld, (Nashville, TN: Abingdon, 2006-) 809.

The Bible affords an especially rich resource for dealing with cultural clash. It exhibits a "culture discourse" in that it "embraces a whole series of different cultures over several millennia, and one can see within the diverse times and places a whole range of possible cultural interactions."[242] Godly culture and ungodly, worldly culture have coexisted since the fall. Before the fall, God's intention was for humanity to rule over all earthly creatures in the three spheres of heaven, land and sea (Gen. 1:26, 28). Humans had freedom to rule as agents of a benevolent God who opposes and subdues evil. Bruce K. Waltke, in *An Old Testament Theology*, notes that:

> [Theologians] refer to the command to subdue the earth and to have dominion over it as the cultural mandate (our blessing and responsibility to develop culture under the lordship of Christ). All human beings are—by nature in their reproducing of themselves and in the shape of what they are—culture makers. . . . The issue is not whether human beings will develop culture; the only issue is what kind? Will it be godly or ungodly? Will it be motivated by agape (God's love) or eros (self-love)? . . . An ungodly, worldly mandate made human beings abuse and violate through their greed and fear, pride and hubris.[243]

In their sinful nature, human beings are tempted to enjoy God's creation yet give the credit to themselves or to someone or something other than the Creator. Cain's lineage is:

> . . . symbolic of human culture with great civilization and no living God . . . and instead of honoring God,

---

[242] Lucien Legrand, *The Bible on Culture* (Maryknoll, NY: Orbis 2000), vii.
[243] Bruce K. Waltke, *An Old Testament Theology* (Grand Rapids, MI: Zondervan, 2007), 220.

the believer honors a human being, naming his city after his son. . . .

The evangelism mandate and the culture mandate coexist to please God . . . so that Christians may enjoy God after they glorify him first.[244]

Pastors should therefore present their whole life to God as a sacrifice, "an offering of one's whole self in the course of one's concrete living, a matter not only of interior thoughts, feelings and aspirations, but also of outward words and deeds, of obedience of life (Rom 12:1)."[245] Charles Talbert adds that Romans 12:2:

> . . . is a parallel exhortation to v.1. If the first focused on us as "bodies," the second concerns ourselves as "minds." Taken together, the emphasis is on the total self-given to God. The first part of the exhortation is negative: "Do not be conformed to this world." [Meaning the present evil age with its distorted values/worldly culture.] A positive follows: "Be transformed by the renewing of your minds" (cf. 3:10; Eph. 4:23). The verbs are passive: "be conformed, be transformed." The self is caught between cosmic powers that struggle for control of life: sin [worldly culture] and God [godly culture]. . . . Those [godly pastors] who have been set free and granted God's enabling presence, however, are capable of a proper response to "do not be conformed" and "be transformed." With a

---

[244] Ibid., 221.
[245] C.E.B. Cranfield, *A Shorter Commentary on the Epistle to the Romans* (Grand Rapids, MI: Eerdmans, 1985), 295.

transformed mind one is able to discern God's will, recognizing it as "good, acceptable, and perfect."[246]

Douglas Moo, in *The Epistle to the Romans*, clarifies further that it is the mercy of God that gives power and stimulates our hearts to obey God's will.[247]

> We experience God's mercy as a power that exerts a total and all-encompassing claim upon us: grace now "reigns" over us (Rom. 5:21). . . . This world, literally "this age" [worldly, ungodly culture], is the sin-dominated, death-producing realm in which all people, included in Adam's fall, naturally belong. But it was "to deliver us from the present evil age" that Christ gave himself (Gal. 1:4); and "those who belong to Christ have been transferred from the old realm of sin and death into the new realm of righteousness and life (Rom 5:17, 21; 6:2-6, 14, 17-18, 22; 7:2-6; 8:2,9).[248]

Commentators also point out the difference between *conform* and *transform* in Romans 12:1-2. Cranfield explains that:

> . . . on the basis of the Gospel, in light of "the mercies of God," there is only one possibility that is properly open to them, and that is to resist this process of being continually molded and fashioned according to the pattern of this present age with its conventions and its standards of values. . . . The

---

[246] Charles H. Talbert, *Romans* (Macon, GA: Smyth & Helwys, 2002), 284-285.
[247] Douglas J. Moo, *The Epistle to the Romans* (Grand Rapids, MI: Eerdmans 1996), 749-50.
[248] Ibid., 755 .

Christian has always to confess that to a painfully large extent his life is conformed to this age. . . . [To establish a godly culture] he is to allow himself to be transformed continually, remolded, and remade, so that his life here and now may more and more clearly exhibit signs and tokens of the coming order of God, that order which has already come in Christ.[249]

Even though we inhabit a new realm, a new culture from the Lord Jesus Christ, we still cope with the influence of the old realm. That is why Paul urged us to "not be conformed to this world," but "be transformed." The tense of both verbs is present which means that the struggle between two cultures is continuous, and "renewing of your mind" is a lifelong process of "approving the will of God."

Thus, to reduce the symptoms of burnout, pastors need to remain aware that the adoption of a godly mindset is a life-long process. As pastors come to understand, agree with and put into practice God's will by following the lead of the Holy Spirit (Rom. 8:4-9), the fallen mind will be renewed; our worldly mind will change from self-centered to others-centered through the practice of obeying God's will, and this in turn will enhance discernment of the will of God.

Jesus commanded his disciples "Be perfect, therefore, as your heavenly Father is perfect" (Matt. 5:48 NIV) Does this mean pastors are to be as sinless, flawless and powerful as the Great Shepherd, Jesus Christ? The Greek word for "perfect" is *teleios*, the equivalent of the Hebrew *tamim*. As Hagner explains, tamim is often used in the Old Testament to refer to perfection "in the sense of ethical uprightness," and this is paralleled by Jesus's call for the disciples to love God, their neighbor, and even their enemies,[250] for the sun rises and the rain falls on the "righteous and the unrighteous." (5:45 NIV)

---

[249] Cranfield, *Romans*, 297.
[250] Donald A. Hagner, *Matthew 1-13* (Dallas, TX: Word, 1993), 135.

In fact, for Blomberg, "perfect" would be better rendered as mature or whole love towards God and human beings,[251] but he asserts that this kind of expectation cannot be fully practiced until the second coming of the Lord/consummation of the Kingdom.[252]

R.T. France agrees that "the demand of the kingdom of heaven has no limit—or rather its limit is perfection, the perfection of God himself"—so this is a clear and present expectation of the disciples.[253] The wording of the summary (5:48) recalls the repeated formula of Leviticus: "Be holy because I, the Lord your God, am holy." (Lev. 19:2b NIV) God's people were to reflect his character; the same holds for contemporary heirs to the kingdom of heaven (Matt. 5:3-10). Jesus' use of *teleios* (perfect) instead of "holy" may derive from the requirement of total loyalty to God in Deuteronomy 18:13. It is a broader term than moral flawlessness and is used to designate spiritual "maturity."[254]

In his research on the nature of perfection in Jesus' teaching, Brad Riddle agrees that perfection in the Bible denotes not absolute moral purity or the absence of sin, but maturity and wholeness: "Jesus' startling and poignant declaration is that kingdom ethics include a love that embraces disciples' enemies and persecutors. Significant scholarly opinion exists that this divine imperative of perfection establishes a goal that will be partially reached on this earth and completely realized in the coming kingdom."[255] Within the framework of Matthew, one message is clear: the imminent arrival of the Kingdom of God. We are in the era of "already but

---

[251] Craig L. Blomberg, *Matthew* (Nashville, TN: Broadman, 1992), 115.

[252] Ibid., 95.

[253] R.T. France, *The Gospel of Matthew* (Grand Rapids, MI: Eerdmans, 2007), 228.

[254] Ibid., 228.

[255] Brad A. Riddle, "Exploring the Effect of a Lifestyle Enrichment Program to Reduce Perfectionism and Increase Spiritual, Individual, and Interpersonal Satisfaction in Christians, Using a Cognitive Behavioral Intervention" (D.Min. diss., Denver Seminary, 2006), 60.

not yet." Larry Helyer asserts that the essence of discipleship for the Kingdom of God is to "take up your cross and follow me [Jesus], die and rise with Christ; and believe and abide in Christ."[256]

Use of the imperatival future tense in Matthew 5:48 NIV ("Be perfect,") suggests that this expectation is not unrealistic. God has not "reduced" this requirement in our pursuit of His perfection or in becoming spiritually mature. He has not set this highest goal only for the disciples, his servants and under-shepherds; pastors are to aim for the goal but also promise followers that to this same end the Lord will be with them until the end of the world.[257] As Wilkins further clarifies, Jesus is not saying "Be spiritually mature as your heavenly Father is mature." For Matthew, the Father is the goal.[258] The injunction "to be perfect" thus implies "an imperfect process that goes on throughout this life and accepts it as a goal that will be fully realized only in the future."[259]

In Matthew 19:16-30, a rich young man came to Jesus seeking eternal life; he believed he had lived a good life, but desired to serve God more. Are such expectations "unrealistic" or godly? Matthew France avers that Jesus is showing the young man the "perfect" standard demanded by the Kingdom of God. He continues to unwrap the deeper spiritual problem of this young man's ambition— he is right to be doing "some more searching." He wants to be "perfect," not so much morally flawless but as with complete or full maturity. That is what Jesus wants for him, too, just as he does for all his disciples, according to Mat. 5:48.[260] Wilkins suggests that Jesus was reaching to the central problem of this young man's life, that his possessions had become his "identity, power, purpose, and

---

[256] Larry R. Helyer, *The Witness of Jesus, Paul, and John: An Exploration in Biblical Theology* (Downers Grove, IL: InterVarsity, 2008), 401

[257]   France, *Matthew*, 254.

[258] Michael J.Wilkins, *The NIV Application Commentary : Matthew* (Grand Rapids, MI : Zondervan, 2004), 255.

[259] Ibid., 267.

[260] France, *Matthew*, 734-35.

meaning in life."[261] Was there an ungodly agenda at the root of such unrealistic expectations for this world? Or are such expectations "perfect" (godly) yet attainable only by the "easy yoke" that Jesus offered, to "Are you tired? Worn out? Burned out on religion? Come to me…" (Matt. 11:28-30 MSG) Presumably the answer is "Yes."

Sheng Ding and Robert A. Saunders trace the evolution of the definition of culture from the 19th to the 21st Centuries:

> As early as 1871, the English anthropologist Edward B. Tylor wrote, "Culture or civilization, defined in its wide ethnographic sense, is that complex whole which includes knowledge, belief, art, morals, law, custom, and any other capabilities and habits acquired by man as a member of society." Entering the 21st century, culture is commonly defined as a "set of distinctive spiritual, material, intellectual and emotional features of society or a social group and that it encompasses, in addition to art and literature, lifestyles, ways of living together, value systems, traditions and beliefs."[262]

Stella Ting-Toomey adds that "culture as a complex frame of reference . . . consists of patterns of traditions, beliefs, values, norms, symbols, and meanings that are shared to varying degrees by interacting members of a community."[263]

Using these criteria for culture, it becomes evident that an individual can be exposed to multiple cultures in a single lifetime, beginning with one's childhood family experience and its stated or

---

[261] Wilkins, *Matthew*, 649.

[262] Sheng Ding and Robert A. Saunders, "Talking up China: An Analysis of China's Rising Cultural Power and Global Promtion of Chinese Language," *East Asia* 23, no. 2 (2006): 5.

[263] Stella Ting-Toomey, *Communicating Across Cultures* (New York: Guilford, 1999), 10.

inferred beliefs and values. It is primarily during adolescent years that increasing exposure to pop culture occurs, with beliefs and values directly or indirectly derived from the entertainment industry or prominent athletes. By attending advanced educational institutions with their varied clubs and societies, an individual is surrounded with still other and even more diverse cultural values and beliefs.

Although not meant to be all-inclusive, the aforementioned examples are cited merely to demonstrate that an individual may be exposed to a wide variety of cultures in his or her lifetime. Unfortunately, the multiple cultures and individual experiences may clash in significant ways. Accepting a pastoral calling but failing to recognize one's prior exposure to these diverse cultural values may impact one's ability to fulfill the pastoral calling. Trying to meet all the varied expectations associated with one's familial, national and racial values creates tensions, anxiety, weariness, depression, and may contribute to burnout and eventually lead to ministry dropout. Understanding the powerful potential impact of cultural clash on burnout, it is therefore essential when accepting a position as pastor to maintain well-grounded beliefs and values concerning the pastorate in general, pastoral leadership in particular, and awareness of one's own admixture of values.

Edgar H. Schein underscores how important it is for a leader to understand the culture in order to find out what occurs in organizations when different subcultures—that is, of the pastor and the congregation—interact. "They must work with each other."[264] He also defines organizational culture as:

> . . . a pattern of shared basic assumptions that the group learned as it solved its problems of external adaptation and internal integration that has worked well enough to be considered valid and, therefore,

---

[264] Edgar H. Schein, *Organizational Culture and Leadership* (San Francisco, CA:Jossey-Bass, 1992), xii.

to be taught to new members as the correct way to perceive, think, and feel in relation to those problems.[265]

According to Schein, there are three levels of culture. These include artifacts (visible but difficult-to-decipher organizational structures and processes), espoused values (strategies, goals, philosophy; that espoused justifications), and basic underlying assumptions (unconscious, taken-for-granted beliefs, perceptions, thoughts, and feelings; the ultimate sources of values and action).[266] Schein continues:

> Culture and leadership are two sides of the same coin in that leaders (pastors) first create cultures when they create groups and organizations. Once cultures exist, they determine the criteria for leadership and thus determine who will or will not be a leader. But if cultures become dysfunctional, it is the unique function of leadership to perceive the functional and dysfunctional elements of the existing culture and to manage cultural evolution and change in such a way that the group can survive in a changing environment.

> The bottom line for leaders is that if they do not become aware of the cultures in which they are embedded, those cultures will manage them. Cultural understanding is desirable for all of us, but it is essential to leaders if they are to lead.[267]

---

[265] Ibid., 13.
[266] Ibid., 17.
[267] Ibid., 15.

Jackie Katy, in his article "Great Expectations," discusses the unrealistic expectations placed on a pastor by the congregation:

> If I've learned anything in thirty-nine years of ministry, it's that congregations have unrealistic expectations of their pastoral families. The man who stands behind the pulpit on Sunday represents God to his congregation and symbolizes a whole system of faith. To add to his burden, he is attributed certain virtues simply because of his position, and then is expected to exemplify them. He is supposed to be a strong leader but not domineering; preach with fervor but not offend; possess great wisdom but be devoid of pride; and study diligently but not neglect the people. In other words, he must be close to perfect.[268]

Adding to the current complexity of expectations in the USA, pastors find themselves attempting to minister to multiple generations at the same time. For example, many contemporary churches attempt to draw from groups including the pre-war generation, war babies, Baby Boomers, Generation-X, and the Millennial/Generation Y. Each generation has its own expectations. For example:

> Churches that have targeted the baby boomers provide quality programs and facilities. They are committed to excellence but do not require blind loyalty. They strive to communicate on a level comparable to that which the baby boomer experiences in the best of the secular world. The church nursery rivals the day-care center down the street for attractiveness and cleanliness. Sermons are

---

[268] Jackie Katy, "Great Expectations," Quiet Waters Ministries Compass, available at http://www.qwaters.org/compass (accessed February 2007).

compelling and credible for the college-educated parishioner who is both well read and well traveled. High standards are maintained, whether in the matter of biblical truth and/or in the quality of Christian fellowship.[269]

Anderson adds that a targeted, trend-watching ministry demands expertise and vision beyond what is traditionally required by the vocation or included in training. Pastors can struggle with their expectations for ministry and the ambiguity of maintaining separate personal and pastoral identities. Many congregations still measure success in institutional terms: attendance, buildings, budgets, and programs.[270] Pastors, therefore, often compare their success with others in theses same terms.

Unrealistic culture-based expectations may cause burned out pastors to drop out spiritually, mentally and emotionally. Even though they are still physically present, they have already switched their thinking from vocation-centered to "only a job." In that case, formal dropout is anticlimactic. Kent and Barbara Hughes discuss this issue:

> [A pastor] left the church and drove some miles to the city dump where he committed everything to the waiting garbage. This young, gifted pastor was determined never to return to the ministry. . . . We are concerned about the morale and survival of those in Christian ministry—pastors often face significant feelings of failure, usually fueled by misguided expectations for success.[271]

---

[269] Leith Anderson, *Dying for Change* (Minneapolis, MN: Bethany House, 1990), 85.

[270] Yuan, response to Chinese pastor interviews (November 2006).

[271] Kent Hughes and Barbara Hughes, *Liberating Ministry from the Success Syndrome* (Wheaton, IL: Tyndale, 1980), 9.

A. W. Tozer offers an excellent summary of these factors:

> This mania to succeed is a good thing perverted. The desire to fulfill the purpose for which we were created is of course a gift from God, but sin has twisted the impulse about and turned it into a selfish lust for first place and top honors. By this lust the whole world of mankind [sic] is driven by a demon, and there is no escape.

Pastors reflect the culture in which they live; therefore, pastors are affected by a dominant cultural condition. In the author of this paper's experience, Chinese pastors are especially not sharing their inner thoughts with others. The cultural importance of never "losing face" keeps Chinese pastors from confiding personal failures with friends or seeking their advice. Pastors tend to have few friends or no friends at all; however, this is not entirely due to their ministry role. It is also due to the culture wherein pastors live and work, which emphasizes individualism, intelligence, and self-sacrifice.[272]

The dynamics of Asian culture are the dominant cultural condition that influence the Chinese pastor. Consequently the pastor's congregation may be blinded by "face" to the fact that he experiences ups and downs. They expect him to remain on a pedestal and not suffer from common human experiences, and this is only aggravated by the culture of western individualism, intelligence, and self-sacrifice.

---

[272] A. W. Tozer, *Born after Midnight* (Harrisburg, PA: Christian Publications, 1959), 57.

Journey to cope with cultural clash

Studying the culture is key to coping with cultural clash. Christian ministers should continue reading the Bible and studying their own culture the rest of their lives.[273] In Acts 17, Paul preaches to the Athenians from Mars Hill and uses a different point of contact with them than with the Jewish people. He showed his sensitivity as a minister of the Gospel of Jesus Christ. Paul followed Jesus's steps in using different methods with different people. The Lord used a different approach with Nicodemus than with the Samaritan woman. Paul, as an apostle of the Gentiles, pointed out that he is flexible to meet different people's perceptions according to their cultures (Col 3:11).

According to a recent Barna Research study, the perception of Christians by outsiders (non-Christians) is shockingly low. Disdain for evangelicals by young outsiders is overwhelming and negative (49 percent). According to David Kinnaman, President of the Barna Research Group and author of *UnChristian: What a New Generation Really Thinks about Christianity*: "Only a small percentage of outsiders strongly believe that labels 'respect, love, hope, and trust' describe Christianity. A minority of outsiders perceives Christianity as genuine and real, as something that makes sense, and as relevant to their life."[274]

Kinnaman lists the six most common perceptions outsiders have of Christianity: Outsiders largely think that Christians say one thing and do another. They believe we do not act consistently with our beliefs. Outsiders often feel more like targets. They feel as if we merely want to get them "saved" and then move on to another accomplishment. Young outsiders largely view Christians as hateful, bigoted, and non-compassionate in their dealings with homosexuals.

---

[273] Samuel D. Rima, *Leading from the Inside Out: The Art of Self Leadership* (Grand Rapids, MI: Baker Books, 2000), 210.

[274] David Kinnaman, *UnChristian: What a New Generation Really Thinks about Christianity*(Grand Rapid, MI:Baker, 2007), 27.

They tend to view Christians as focused on "curing" homosexuals and using political means to silence them. Outsiders largely think that Christians have simplistic answers to the deep complexities of life. Christians are often viewed as synonymous with right-wing Republican conservatives. Nearly 90 percent of outsiders say that the term "judgmental" accurately describes Christians today. Only 20 percent of outsiders view the church as a place where people are accepted and loved unconditionally.[275] It is crucial that Christian ministers are spiritually discerning about the current trends of culture that are affecting the body of Christ.

Since we are now living in a global village, communicating across cultures is another must for pastors, missionaries and church planners. For example, Asians have a rich culture of "saving face." Spending time to understand the meaning of "face," "face saving" and "face giving" will provide a solid, sensitive cross-culture relationship:

> "Face is a communicator's claim to be seen as a certain type of person; the positive social value a person claims for him or herself. Two dimensions of face can be distinguished. Positive face refers to a person's desire to gain the approval of others; this dimension has two subcomponents: the need to be included and the need to be respected. Negative face refers to the desire to have autonomy and not be controlled by others.

People lose face when their identity claims are challenged or ignored by others. Mutual acknowledgement and cooperative maintenance of face is one of the major concerns in everyday interaction. Challenges to face—which may occur during conflicts and other non-routine episodes—are unusual and threatening. This

---

[275] Ibid., 185.

threatening experience can drive conflicts in negative directions. Face-saving behavior represents attempts by the party to save or to restore face. Face-saving is a major source of inflexibility in conflicts.

Face-giving occurs when parties support others' face claims and work with them to prevent loss of face or to restore face. Corrective and preventive face-giving can be distinguished. Corrective face-giving occurs after loss of face, whereas defensive face-giving is intended to prevent loss of face in the first place."[276]

D.A. Carson, in his book *Christ and Culture Revisited*, emphasizes that we can compare and contrast with other cultures based on particular aspects of Christianity. "The Christian heritage of meanings and values turns on disclosure from God that makes us look at everything differently." Carson also quotes C.S.Lewis: "I believe in Christianity as I believe that the Sun has risen, not only because I see it, but because by it I see everything else."[277] He asks: "What are some of the pressures that force thoughtful Christians to wrestle with how we ought to relate to the broader culture of which we are a part, even if we are a distinguishable part? We are dealing with something that can be an enormous force for good, if firmly embedded within the normative structure of the Bible's story line and priorities. The tensions between Christ and culture are both diverse and complex, but from a Christian perspective they find their origin in the stubborn refusal of human beings, made in God's image, to acknowledge their creaturely dependence on their Maker."[278]

Church ministers either develop the ministry culture or adapt and become part of the established ministry culture. A congregation's culture can help determine whether a pastor's goals can be reached.

---

[276] Joseph P. Folger, Marshall Scott Poole and Randall K. Stutman, *Working through conflict* (New York:Longman, 2001), 182-4.
[277] D.A. Carson, *Christ and Culture Revisited* (Grand Rapids, Michigan:Eerdmans, 2008), 86.
[278] Ibid., 207.

Pastors with cultural sensitivity find out the key values in the churches they serve so they can make appropriate changes.

In *Organizational Culture and Leadership*, Edgar H. Schein argues that leaders create and modify cultures:

> Culture and leadership are two sides of the same coin in which leaders first create cultures when they create groups and organizations. Once cultures exist, they determine the criteria for leadership and thus determine who will or will not be a leader. But if cultures become dysfunctional, it is the unique function of leadership to perceive the functional and dysfunctional elements of the existing culture and to manage cultural evolution and change in such a way that the group can survive in a changing environment. The bottom line for leaders is that if they do not become conscious of the cultures in which they are embedded, those cultures will manage them. . . . Cultural understanding is desirable for all of us, but it is essential to leaders if they are to lead.[279]

Schein's work can apply to pastoral leadership. Pastors who view many problems in the church simply as "communication failures" or "lack of teamwork" should understand these issues as possible breakdowns in inter*cultural* communication.[280]

Organizational culture can be analyzed at three levels. The first level considers visible artifacts such as the organization's architecture, language, creations, myths and stories. The second level seeks to understand the "expounded values."[281] These are the values that lay

---

[279] Edgar H. Schein, *Organizational Culture and Leadership* (San Francisco: Jossey-Bass, 2004), 15.

[280] Ibid., xii.

[281] Ibid.

out the rules and behavioral norms of the group's strategies, goals and philosophies. Expounded values "predict well enough what people [are] willing [to do] in a variety of situations, but which may be out of line with what they will actually do in situations where their values should, in fact, be operating."[282] The third level analyzes an organization's underlying assumptions. These unconscious, taken-for-granted beliefs "guide behavior and tell group members how to perceive, think about and feel about things."[283] Schein writes:

> Cultural assumptions evolve around all aspects of a group's relationship to its external environment. The group's ultimate mission, goals and means used to achieve goals, measurements of its performance, and remedial strategies all require consensus if the group is to perform effectively. If there is conflict between subgroups that form subcultures, such conflict can undermine group performance.

> On the other hand, if the environmental context is changing, such conflict can be a potential source of adaptation and new learning. Degree of consensus is more functional in the early growth of the group. Ultimately, all organizations are sociotechnical systems in which the manner or external adaptation and the solution of internal integration problems are interdependent.[284]

The following are the elements that constitute a successful strategy for establishing a viable, working culture within an organization:

---

282 Ibid., 12.
283 Ibid., 22.
284 Ibid., 68.

1. **Coping cycle—mission and strategy:** This includes obtaining a shared understanding of the core mission, primary tasks, and manifest and/or latent functions.
2. **Goals:** The organization has developed a consensus on goals, as derived from the core mission.
3. **Means:** The organization has also developed a consensus on the means to be used to attain the goals, such as the organization's structure, division of labor, reward system and authority system.
4. **Measurement:** Clear metrics and criteria have been established to be used in measuring how well the group is doing in fulfilling its goals.
5. **Corrections:** The organization has developed a consensus on the appropriate remedial or repair strategies to be used if goals are not being met.[285]

While a group successfully adapts to its external environment, it must also develop and maintain a set of internal relationships among its members. Schein writes:

> The most important conclusion to be derived from this analysis is that culture is a multidimensional, multifaceted phenomenon, not easily reduced to a few major dimensions. Culture ultimately reflects the group's effort to cope and learn and is the residue of the learning process. Culture thus fulfills not only the function of providing stability, meaning and predictability in the present, but is the result of functionally effective decisions in the group's past. The implications for leadership are several. First, the external issues described in this chapter are usually the leader's primary concern because it's the leader

---

[285] Ibid., 52.

who creates the group and wants it to succeed. Even if the group precedes the leader historically, it will generally put one of its members into the leadership role to worry about external boundary management, survival, and growth.

Second, the successful management of these several functions is usually the basis on which leaders are assessed. If they cannot create a group that succeeds, they are considered to have failed as leaders. Internal dissent can be forgiven, but a leader who fails in the external functions is usually abandoned, voted out or gotten rid of in a more dramatic way. . . . The steps of the coping cycle and the issues groups face thus make a useful checklist against which leaders can assess their own performance.[286]

Schein notes that every group must deal with six major internal integration issues:

1. Developing a common language and category system that clearly defines what things mean.
2. Reaching consensus on the boundaries of the group—who is in and who is not in.
3. Developing consensus on how to distribute influence and power so that aggression can counteractively be channeled and formal strategies accurately determined.
4. Developing rules that define peer relationships and intimacy so that love and affection can be appropriately channeled.

---

[286] Ibid., 68-69.

Chi Eng Yuan

5. Developing clear assumptions about what is a reward and what is a punishment so that the group members can decipher how they are doing.
6. Developing explanations that help members deal with unpredictable and unexplainable events. [287]

Schein writes:

The assumptions that develop around these issues constitute (along with assumptions about mission, goals, means, result detection and correction mechanisms) a set of dimensions along which one can study and describe a culture. These are not necessarily the only dimensions one could use but they have the advantage of being tied to a large body of research on groups and permit one to begin to get a sense of the dynamics of culture—how cultural assumptions begin and evolve. They also represent a conceptual grid into which one can store cultural data that one observes. [288]

In short, the entire mechanism is a process with two interdependent sub-processes. According to Schein, there are three stages in the life of an organization. First, the *organizational* stage describes a group's founding and early development. Here the change mechanisms involve incremental change through general and specific evolution. Change might occur through insights from organizational therapy, or it may flow from promotion of hybrids within the organization's culture itself. [289]

Schein explains that early group life tends toward intolerance of animosity and dissent. In the early life of any new organization, one can see many examples of how partners or co-founders who do not think alike end up in conflicts that result in some people leaving, thus creating a more homogeneous climate for those who remain.

---

[287] Ibid
[288] Ibid., 682.
[289] Ibid.

If the original founders do not have proposals to solve the problems that make the group anxious, other strong members will step in and new leaders will emerge. The important point to recognize is that the anxiety of group formation is typically high and covers so many areas of group functioning that leadership is highly sought by group members. If the founder does not succeed in reducing the group's anxiety, other leaders will be empowered by the group.[290]

Founder leaders tend to have strong theories of how to do things, and their theories get tested early. If their assumptions are wrong, the group fails early in its history; however, if their assumptions are correct, they create a powerful organization whose culture reflects the original assumptions.

Christian ministers can use this understanding to determine the readiness for change of the ministry in which they're involved, then quantify their findings with the following 17-point questionnaire developed by Aubrey Malphurs, Ph.D.

Directions:

Each item below is a key element that will help you to evaluate your church's readiness for change. Strive for objectivity and involve others (including outsiders) in the evaluation process. Consider each question and then circle the number from the choices below each question that most accurately rates your church. After answering all 17, evaluate your score according to the following key:

1. Leadership: If the pastor and the church board (official leadership) are enthusiastic about and directly responsible for change, and if any *unofficial* leadership (influential parties such as a church patriarch or wealthy member) is also favorable to change, score 5. If only moderately so, score 3. If only the secondary level of leadership

---

[290] Ibid.

(other staff, Sunday school teachers and so on) is inclined toward change, while unofficial leadership opposes it, score 1.

5 3 1

2. Vision: If the pastor and the board have a single, clear vision of a significant future that looks different from the present, and the pastor is able to mobilize most relevant parties (other staff, boards and the congregation) for action, score 5. If the pastor but not the board envisions a different direction for the church, score 3. If the pastor and board have not thought about a vision, and/or they do not believe that it is important, score 1.

5 3 1

3. Values: If the church's philosophy of ministry (its core values) includes a preference for innovation and creativity; and, though proven forms, methods, and techniques are not discarded at a whim, the church is more concerned with the effectiveness of its ministries than adherence to traditions, score 5. If moderately so, score 3. If the church's ministry forms and techniques have changed little over the years, while its ministry effectiveness has diminished, score 1.

5 3 1

4. Motivation: If the pastor and the board have a strong sense of urgency for change that is shared by the congregation, and if the congregational culture emphasizes the need for constant improvement, score 3. If the pastor and/or the board (most of whom have been in their positions for many years), along with the congregation, are bound by long-standing traditions that are change-resistant and discourage risk-taking, score 1. If your church's culture falls somewhere in between, score 2.

3 2 1

5. Organizational context: How does a change effort affect the other programs in the church (Christian education, worship, missions and so on)? If the individuals in charge are all working together for improvement and innovation, score 3. If only some are, score 2. If many are opposed to change and/or are in conflict with one another over change, score 1.

3 2 1

6. Processes/functions: Major changes in a church almost always require redesigning processes and functions in all the ministries of the church, such as Christian education, church worship and the like. If most in charge of these areas are open to such change, score 3. If only some are, score 2. If most are turf protectors or put their areas of ministry ahead of the church as a whole, score 1.

3 2 1

7. Ministry awareness: Does the leadership of your church keep up with what is taking place in the innovative evangelical churches in the community and across America in terms of ministry and outreach effectiveness? Does it objectively compare what it is doing to the actions of similar churches? If the answer is yes, score 3. If the answer is sometimes, score 2. If no, score 1.

3 2 1

8. Community focus: Does the church know and understand the people in the community -- their needs, hopes, aspirations? Does it stay in direct contact with them? Does it regularly seek to reach them? If the answers are yes, score 3. If only moderately so, score 2. If the church is not in touch with its community and focuses primarily on itself, score 1.

3 2 1

9. Evaluation: Does the church regularly evaluate its ministries? Does it evaluate its ministries in light of its vision and goals? Are these ministries regularly adjusted in response to those evaluations? If all of this takes place, score 3. If some takes place, score 2. If none, score 1.

3 2 1

10. Rewards: Change is easier if the leaders and those involved in ministry are rewarded in some way for taking risks and looking for new solutions to their ministry problems. Also, rewarding ministry teams is more effective than rewarding solo performances. If this characterizes your church, score 3. If some times, score 2. If your church rewards the status quo and only a maintenance mentality, score 1.

3 2 1

11. Organizational structure: The best situation is a flexible church where change is well received and takes place periodically. If this is true of your church, score 3. Some churches are very rigid in their structure and either have changed very little in the last five years or have experienced several futile attempts at change to no avail. If this describes your church, score 1. If yours is somewhere in between, score 2.

3 2 1

12. Communication: Does your church have a variety of means for two-way communication? Do most understand and use it, and does it reach all levels of the congregation? If true, score 3. If only moderately true, score 2. If communication is poor, primarily one-way and top-down, score 1.

3 2 1

13. Organizational hierarchy: Is your church decentralized (has few if any levels of leadership between the congregation and the pastor or the board)? If so, score 3. If there are staff levels, boards or committees that come between the congregation and the pastor or board, creating more potential to inhibit essential change, score 1. If between these extremes, score 2.

3 2 1

14. Prior change: Churches will most readily adapt to change if they have successfully implemented major changes in the recent past. If your church has, score 3. If it has succeeded with minor changes, score 2. If no one can remember the last time the church changed or if such efforts failed or left people angry and resentful, score 1.

3 2 1

15. Morale: Do the church staff and volunteers enjoy the church and take responsibility for their ministries? Do they trust the pastor and/or the board? If so, score 3. If moderately so, score 2. Do few people volunteer and are there signs of low team spirit? Is there mistrust between leaders and followers and between the various ministries? If so, score 1.

3 2 1

16. Innovation: Does your church try new things? Do its people feel free to implement new ideas on a consistent basis. Do they have the freedom to make choices and solve problems regarding their ministries? If yes to all, score 3. If this is somewhat true, score 2. If ministries are snared in bureaucratic red tape and permission from "on high" must be obtained before anything happens, score 1.

3 2 1

17. Decision-making: Does your church leadership listen carefully to a wide variety of suggestions from a wide variety of the congregation? After it has gathered the appropriate information, does it make decisions quickly? If so, score 3. If moderately so, score 2. Does leadership listen only to a select few and take forever to make a decision? Is there significant conflict during the process and, after a decision is made, is there confusion and turmoil? Score 1

3 2 1

Your church's total score: _____

Evaluation key: If your score is . . .

47-57: The chances are good that your church may implement change, especially if your scores are high on items 1-3.

28-46: Change may take place but with varying success. Chances increase the higher the score on items 1-3. Note areas with low scores and focus on improvement before attempting change on a large scale.

17-27: Change will not likely take place. Note areas with low scores and attempt to improve them, if possible. Consider starting a new church and implement your ideas in a more "change-friendly" context.

With an understanding of cultural differences, Christian ministers may spend time reflecting on the family, society and church culture in which they grew up, while analyzing the ministries and the culture of the community in which they participate. The habitual practice of cultural discernment against a Scriptural background will sharpen the minister's mind-set and increase his or her depth of cultural understanding—before seeking cultural change—after a clear understanding of God's will in that period of their life.

This questionnaire is designed for the pastors/ministers, who felt spiritually burning away from their works, to measure the frequency and intensity of spiritual burnout on a scale of 0 to 6 scores (0 = never; 1 = a few times in a year; 2 = once a month; 3 = a few times in a month; 4 = once a week; 5 = a few times in a week; and 6 = every day).

1. Spiritual Dryness
   1. I feel spiritually drained from my ministry/workplace.
   2. I do not have enough time to study the Bible.
   3. I do not have enough time to pray and to meditate.
   4. I do not have enough time to spend time with God.
   5. I spend less time alone with God by choice.
   6. I neglect my own spiritual growth.
   7. I become increasingly judgmental and I lose joy in ministry/workplace.
   8. I serve God for my own ambitions rather than love for God
   9. I seem powerless to control the sinful desires.

2. Incompatibility
   1. I believe myself to be inferior to, and incapable of, fulfilling my role as a minister/job title (designation) exactly.
   2. I feel incompetent when facing demands and challenges.
   3. I feel that I have difficult time to take my responsibility.
   4. I am incompatible with my ministry/job description.
   5. I do not fit in with the organization of my current ministry/ profession.
   6. I do not meet the needs of the people who are ministered by my ministry/at workplace.

3. Lack of a Personal Confidant
   1. I do not have a close confidant/friend to support me.
   2. I have difficulty to find an authentic friendship.
   3. I feel lonely among the people who are ministered by my ministry/at workplace.
   4. I feel distant with the people who are ministered by my ministry/at workplace.
   5. I psychologically disguised my actual inner feelings when I relate to others.
   6. I like to play my role in my minister/workplace without touching upon my real self.
   7. I have difficulty in finding people to talk with about personal issues.
   8. I do not have any friend.
   9. I do not have enough time for friends.
   10. I have lost the sense of connection with others.
   11. I hold my title rather than a call to be a minister/a call to do something.

4. Culture Clash
   1. I'm exposed to a variety of dissimilar cultures.
   2. I accept the calling to be a minister but I fail to recognize my prior exposure to these diverse cultural values.
   3. The origin of my client's family and their culture are different from mine.
   4. The multiple cultures I experienced clashing in significant ways.
   5. The culture factors of my ministry/work place is seriously collided with that of mine.
   6. The different subcultures in my ministry/work place do not work with each other.
   7. The unreality of people's expectations has overloaded on my ministry/workplace.

5. Insufficient Rest
   1. I view my calling as a whole day, 24-hour/7-work hour commitment.
   2. People view my calling as a whole day, 24-hour/7-work hour commitment.
   3. I usually deny the duty to care for myself.
   4. I am used to working overtime.
   5. I feel futile if I have spare time.
   6. I have a fear of whether I am able to sidestep the hardship when I am busy.
   7. I tend not to know how to relax.

6. Dysfunctional Conflict Management
   1. I have at least one serious conflict with one of the tasks in my ministry /workplace.
   2. I do not know how to keep better relationship with others in my ministry/workplace.
   3. I prefer avoid focusing on the issue of resolving the conflict.
   4. I do not know how to perceive and make use of emotion to affect relationship with others.
   5. I do not know how to manage the conflict.
   6. I do not know how to control my anger.

If you have find out that you have average 4 in one or more areas, you burn out. Do not be worried. I have prayed for you the time I'm working for this questionnaire and please follow the advice to burn for Christ but just…do not burnout.

Printed in the United States
By Bookmasters